SPACE
RECORD
BREAKERS

THIS IS A CARLTON BOOK

© Carlton Books Limited 2014, 2019

Senior Editor: Alexandra Koken
Design Manager: Jake da'Costa
Design: room9design
Cover Design: Jake da'Costa
Consultant: Raman Prinja
Production: Marion Storz

This edition published 2019 by Carlton Books Limited
An imprint of the Carlton Publishing Group
20 Mortimer Street, London W1T 3JW

2 4 6 8 10 9 7 5 3 1

A catalogue record for this book is available
from the British Library.

ISBN: 978-1-78312-445-9

Printed in Dubai

SPACE RECORD BREAKERS

ANNE ROONEY

CARLTON KiDS

🏆 ABOUT THE AUTHOR

Anne Rooney has written more than 150 books for young (and older) people, many of them on different aspects of science and technology. She has never left Earth, but is made entirely from atoms created billions of years ago in distant stars.

CONTENTS

SPACE RECORD BREAKERS

★ ★ ★ ★ ★ ★

RECORD-BREAKING
SPACE

The universe: it's the biggest thing there is, the oldest thing there is, and everything there is. It's the ultimate record breaker! Most of the universe is space — so space is full of record breakers.

The universe is all of space and time, all the matter and energy we know of. We don't know where it came from or how it will end, and we don't even know what most of it is. What we do know is that the universe is full of fascinating mysteries, waiting to be uncovered.

STARTING WITH A BANG

Scientists believe the universe started with the Big Bang – the biggest bang there has ever been – though there wasn't any sound. In a tiny fraction of a second, something the size of an atom exploded at an unimaginably high temperature (about 10^{32} °C/ about 50^{32} °F) and started expanding to become the entire universe. Just a millionth of a second later, the cooling universe was 10^{13} °C/ 50^{13}°F, and began making the building blocks of atoms. After three minutes, the universe was a huge, dark fog, still super-hot at 10^9 (1 billion) °C (about 50^9°F). In those first moments, the universe was expanding faster than the speed of light!

FIRST THINGS FIRST

Atomic nuclei of helium and hydrogen formed after the first few minutes, but it took 300,000 years for the universe to cool enough (to about 10,000 °C/ about 18,032 °F) for the first atoms to appear. There was light for the first time, too, as the fog of energy cleared into atoms and empty space, and photons — tiny parcels of light energy — could travel through it.

OLDEST GALAXIES

As vast clouds of gas developed, gravity made them collapse inwards, forming galaxies of early stars. The oldest observed galaxies are just over 13 billion years old. The light we see from these early galaxies left from them 13 billion years ago, so we are seeing the galaxies as they were less than a billion years after the universe began. There may be even older ones we haven't seen.

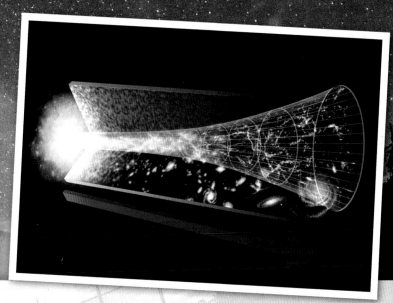

STILL GROWING

The universe is still expanding from the Big Bang. We know this because the space between galaxies is growing, pushing them further apart. That means that we can't see or measure the things that are furthest away as the light from them hasn't had time to reach us yet. No one knows for certain whether the universe will expand and cool forever (most likely), stop expanding at some point, or collapse back in on itself.

MORE RECORD-BREAKING SPACE

SPACE IS LUMPY

Space is mostly empty, but it also contains billions of galaxies, or systems of stars — some with planets. Galaxies have all been produced by gravity drawing matter together.

All matter exerts gravity, pulling other matter and energy towards it. The more mass an object has, the more gravity it exerts. Stars and planets pull themselves together, creating 'lumps' or 'clusters' in empty space. At the same time, the impact of the Big Bang is still pushing everything in the universe further apart and making the universe expand.

YOU'RE A STAR!

Each star in the universe is a searingly hot ball of gases undergoing nuclear fusion. In stars, the heavier atoms are forged from hydrogen and helium. Your body is made of atoms, and all atoms were made in stars — so all the atoms in your body were formed in stars billions of years ago!

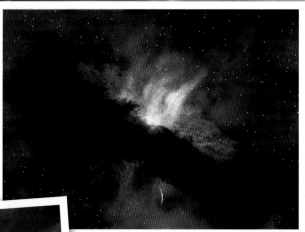

THE UNIVERSE	
AGE	13.8 BILLION YEARS
MASS	PERHAPS 10^{50}–10^{53} KG (22^{50}–22^{53} LB)
DIAMETER	AT LEAST 93 BILLION LIGHT YEARS

Stellar nebula

Average star

Red giant

Planetary nebula

White dwarf

Massive star

Red supergiant

Supernova

Neutron star

Black hole

🪐 MOST SPECTACULAR DEATHS

Stars have a predictable life cycle, though what happens to them depends on their mass. Massive stars (stars that have a lot of mass) have the most spectacular deaths of anything in the universe. They grow larger and hotter as they age, turning into a red supergiant — a huge star that glows red. Then they explode in a spectacular supernova event, which leaves behind a neutron star or a black hole. Less massive stars first become a red giant and then a planetary nebula: a huge cloud of electrically-charged gas. All that is left afterwards is a white dwarf — a very dense, faintly glowing remnant of a dead star.

🪐 MOST PUZZLING MYSTERIES

There's a lot we know about the universe, but more we don't. What we know explains only a tiny fragment of the universe — around 5%. More than a fifth of the universe is made up of what we call 'dark matter', which we can't see because it doesn't reflect or emit light. Most astronomers think of it is a special kind of matter we haven't discovered yet, rather than matter of a familiar type that is behaving differently. Nearly three quarters of the universe is so-called 'dark energy' we know nothing about. Space is a pretty puzzling subject!

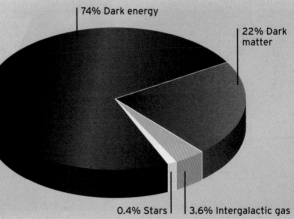

74% Dark energy

22% Dark matter

0.4% Stars

3.6% Intergalactic gas

NEAREST STAR

THE SUN

The Sun, blazing so brightly that it provides all the light on Earth, is our nearest star. Like other stars, it is a scorching hot ball of gas, producing energy from a process called 'nuclear fusion'.

The Sun rotates on its axis, taking 25 Earth days to turn once. Our whole solar system, with the Sun at its centre, whirls through space around the centre of our galaxy, the Milky Way. Although the Sun travels at 222 km (138 miles) per second, it takes 200 million years to complete one orbit around the centre of the Milky Way.

The Sun is 8 light minutes from Earth — so it takes 8 minutes for light leaving the Sun to reach us.

lar wind is a stream particles that form sma. The particles vel at more than 0 km (249 miles) second — fast ough to leave the n and blast off o space.

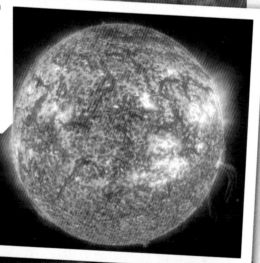

 ## BURNING UP

Nuclear fusion happens in the Sun's core, where hydrogen atoms are forced together under immense pressure, producing helium. The process releases energy in different forms of radiation, including visible, ultraviolet and infrared light, X-rays, microwaves and radio waves. At about 4.5 billion years old, the Sun is halfway through its life. It will gradually heat up and grow larger, burning out all life on Earth, and then shrink to a white dwarf.

LIFE CYCLE OF THE SUN

YOU ARE HERE   GRADUAL WARMING

BIRTH   1   2   3   4   5   6

THE SOLAR SYSTEM

Our Earth and the seven planets in our solar system orbit the Sun. But that's not all. There are also asteroids and other small objects, including dwarf planets and comets, orbiting the Sun. The gravitational pull of the Sun keeps the planets in orbit, preventing them from whizzing off into space.

Earth

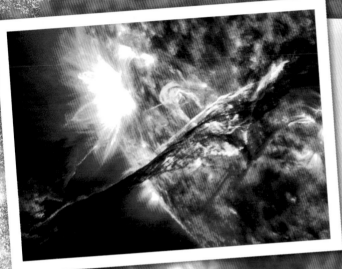

ACTIVE SUN

The Sun blasts solar wind out into space and solar flares leap from the surface in dramatic bursts. The wind and flares are made up of tiny charged particles, mostly electrons and protons. The wind gets weaker as it gets further from the Sun. Solar wind can push as far as a point called the 'heliopause', where stray particles and dust that make up the 'interstellar medium', become stronger than the solar wind.

The surface temperature is 6,000 °C (10,832 °F) and the temperature at the core is 15,700,000 °C (28,260,032 °F).

THE SUN

AGE	4.6 BILLION YEARS
MASS	1.99 X 10³⁰ KG (4.4 X 10³⁰ LB) (330,000 X EARTH)
DIAMETER	1,392,000 KM (864,949 MILES) (10⁹ X EARTH)
DISTANCE FROM EARTH	147,000,000-152,000,000 KM (91,341,565-94,448,421 MILES) (1 AU)
REMAINING LIFE	5 BILLION YEARS

RED GIANT   PLANETARY NEBULA   WHITE DWARF

8   9   10   11   11.001   12   13

BILLIONS OF YEARS [APPROX.]

BEST METEOR SHOWER

PERSEID METEOR SHOWER

Each year, hundreds of brilliant meteors flash through the night sky as they plunge towards Earth. The Perseid meteor shower, visible mid-July to mid-August, provides most of the meteors seen each year.

Meteorites are chunks of rock or metal (or both) that fall to Earth from space. While they are in space they are called meteors. As they drop through the atmosphere they glow brightly, making a streak across the sky. We also call these shooting stars, or falling stars.

A chunk of rock travelling at 58 km (36 miles) per second hurtles towards the Earth, burning brightly as the friction with the atmosphere heats and slows it down.

 ## ROCK OF AGES

Many meteors are the debris of crashes between asteroids, which date from the formation of the solar system, so they're more than 4 billion years old. Others are lumps knocked off the Moon or Mars. Those from the Moon are 2.5 billion years old and those from Mars can be very young, at just 65 million years old.

METEORS FROM A COMET

The comet Swift-Tuttle has a 133-year orbit around the Sun. Each orbit leaves a trail of debris in its wake, and the Perseids come from that. Every year, as Earth passes through the debris left behind by Swift-Tuttle on its previous orbits, small fragments of rock are caught up by Earth's gravity and dragged towards it.

Sixty or more meteors per hour are visible at the height of the Perseids' activity.

A trail of burning gas glows behind the meteor as it streaks through the sky, each one visible for just a second or two.

COULD YOU BE HIT BY A METEORITE?

It's very rare to be hit by a meteorite! A few people claim they have been, but no one is known to have been killed by a meteorite. But in 1992, 17-year-old Michelle Knapp's car was badly dented by the Peekskill meteorite in New York State, USA. The 4.4-billion-year-old chunk of rock weighed 12 kg (26.5 lb) and measured 30 cm (11.8 in) across.

PERSEID METEOR SHOWER

DATE FIRST RECORDED	36 AD
METEORS PER HOUR	AROUND 60
SPEED OF METEORITES	210,000 KM/H (130,488 MPH)

FIRST MAN-MADE OBJECT IN SPACE

A-4 ROCKET

The A-4 rocket, launched on 3 October 1942, was the first man-made object to go into space. Reaching an altitude of 96.5 km (60 miles), the rocket just entered space (which officially starts 80 km (50 miles) above sea level).

Its inventor, Wernher von Braun, wanted to make a rocket for space exploration, but the Second World War had started so instead it was developed for warfare. The A-4 travelled faster than sound, so it could drop bombs silently: the sound of it roaring through the air arrived only after the bomb's impact.

14 m (46 ft) long, the A-4 could travel a distance of 377 km (234 miles) from launch.

 SPACE OR WAR?

For a while, Wernher von Braun was taken off the A-4 project because he wanted to pursue the 'fantasy' of his rocket going into Earth's orbit or visiting the Moon. After a successful bombing mission (right), von Braun remarked, "The rocket worked perfectly except for landing on the wrong planet." After the war, he and his team surrendered to the USA and he led rocket development at NASA.

FASTER THAN SOUND

Sound is produced by waves of pressure in the air hitting the eardrum. The speed of sound in air is 340 m (1,115.5 feet) per second. When something travels faster than sound, we hear a crack or boom as it breaks the sound barrier, then the object travels ahead of its own sound, so we see it before we hear it. When aircraft such as the FA-18 Hornet (right) break the sound barrier, there is no sound as there are no air molecules to vibrate.

The 72,500 kg (159,835 lb) thrust produces a top upward speed of 1,340 m (4,396 feet) per second.

3,400 injection ports mixed 58 kg (128 lb) of alcohol-mix and 72 kg (159 lb) of oxygen for burning every second. It burned for 65-70 seconds before shutting down.

A-4 ROCKET (LATER RENAMED V-2)

DATE	1942
TOP SPEED	4,825 KM/H (2,998 MPH)
GROUND IMPACT SPEED	3,240-3,600 KM/H (2,013-2,237 MPH)
DISTANCE TRAVELLED	377 KM (234 MILES)
ALTITUDE	96.5 KM (60 MILES)

IT'S ROCKET SCIENCE

A rocket works by producing a massive boost of energy by burning fuel under high pressure. It's effectively an explosion in a small space. The hot gases produced by the burning fuel are forced out of the back of the rocket, pushing the rocket forward with immense force.

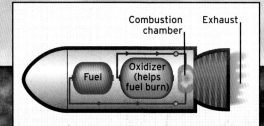

Combustion chamber   Exhaust

Fuel   Oxidizer (helps fuel burn)

BEST TELESCOPE

HUBBLE TELESCOPE

The Hubble Space Telescope is a huge telescope permanently based in space. It orbits Earth, beaming stunningly vivid photos of all parts of the universe back to us. It was carried into space by the space shuttle Discovery.

Mirrors inside Hubble collect visible and ultraviolet light as well as infrared radiation. Computers make images of near and deep space from the data. Hubble has sent hundreds of thousands of images back to Earth, revealing amazing information about the history and nature of the universe. They have helped us to work out the age of the universe: about 13.7 billion years.

Solar panels collect energy to power the telescope's instruments.

If the Hubble telescope could be focused on objects on Earth, it would be able to see objects just 30cm (11.8 in) across! (It can't do it, because the Earth reflects too much light.)

SEEING IN SPACE

Even the biggest and most powerful telescopes on Earth can't produce such clear and precise images as a telescope in space. Earth's atmosphere limits what telescopes on Earth can do. Light is distorted as it passes through our atmosphere, and some types of radiation are blocked completely by it. Positioning a telescope above the atmosphere avoids these problems.

Antennae enable Hubble to communicate with mission control on Earth, where hundreds of scientists work to keep it operational and control its work.

 FANTASY IMAGES

Hubble has given us photos of things never seen before, from towering dust columns a trillion km (over 600 billion miles) tall where stars are made, to the faint glimmer of dying stars. When Hubble was set to watch an area that looked like empty space, it found thousands of new galaxies, billions of light years away. It doesn't only show where there are stars — it shows where there aren't, searching for black holes and dark matter.

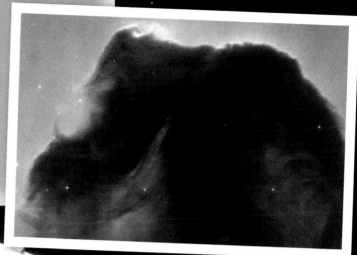

HUBBLE SPACE TELESCOPE

LAUNCH DATE	1990
SIZE	13.2 M (43 FT) LONG, 4.2 M (14 FT) DIAMETER
ALTITUDE	569 KM (354 MILES)
ORBITAL PERIOD	97 MINUTES
SPEED	8 KM/SECOND (5 MILES/ SECOND) - 28,800 KM/H (17,896 MPH)

HOW FAR CAN WE SEE?

Light travels at nearly 300,000 km (186,411 miles) per second. A light year is the distance light can travel in a year – about 9,500,000,000,000 km (nearly 6 trillion miles). When we look at galaxies millions of light years away, we see them as they were millions of years ago. Hubble sees back in time up to 13.2 billion years!

NEAREST NEIGHBOUR

THE MOON

The Moon is Earth's only natural satellite and nearest neighbour. Its surface is pitted with craters caused by impacts from lumps of rock hurtling through space. Over billions of years, the entire surface has been blasted to dust and rubble.

As far as we know, the Moon has never been home to any life forms. There is no liquid water, only water trapped as ice within the surface, and only the thinnest atmosphere surrounds it. It's an inhospitable place that can't support life as we know it.

Dark areas called 'maria' (seas) are fairly flat planes of lava that filled impact craters between 4.2 and 1.2 billion years ago and then hardened.

NEW MOON, FULL MOON

From Earth, the Moon appears to change shape from a crescent moon to the round full moon, and back again, as its position in relation to Earth and the Sun changes. When the Moon is full, the side facing Earth is fully illuminated by the Sun.

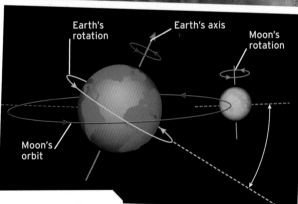

Earth's rotation

Earth's axis

Moon's rotation

Moon's orbit

The Moon orbits the Earth once every 27.3 days and turns on its own axis once in the same time.

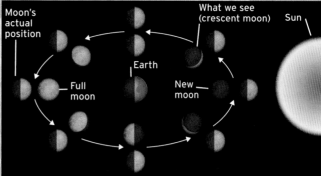

Moon's actual position

What we see (crescent moon)

Sun

Earth

Full moon

New moon

THE MOON'S DARK SIDE

The part of the Moon which faces the Earth while it is illuminated by the Sun is always the same side. The other side, sometimes called the dark side of the Moon but more sensibly called the far side, is never seen from Earth because when it faces us, it's dark. We now know what it looks like because it has been photographed from space.

The far side of the Moon has fewer maria and more craters — maria cover 31% of the near side but only 1% of the far side.

HOW TO MAKE A MOON

The best theory for how the Moon formed is that a large rocky body about the size of Mars crashed into Earth about 4.5 billion years ago, blasting off part of Earth. Scorching-hot molten debris from both Earth and whatever hit it clumped together and cooled, spinning itself into a sphere at the same time, making the Moon.

THE MOON

DISCOVERY	PREHISTORIC
FIRST DETAILED OBSERVATION	1610, GALILEO
DISTANCE FROM EARTH	384,400 KM (238,855 MILES)
DIAMETER	3,475 KM (2,159 MILES) ($\frac{1}{4}$ OF EARTH)
MASS	7.35 X 10^{22} KG (16 X 10^{22} LB (0.012 OF EARTH)
ORBITAL VELOCITY	1,023 M/SECOND (3,683 KM/H)

FIRST MANNED SPACE FLIGHT

VOSTOK 1

In 1961, Vostok 1, with cosmonaut Yuri Gagarin on board, made a single orbit of the Earth. The flight took only 108 minutes and remains the shortest-ever manned orbit.

Vostok 1 had no back-up rockets. In case the single retro-rocket needed to send it back to Earth failed, there was a ten-day supply of food to keep Yuri Gagarin going until the orbit decayed and Vostok fell back to Earth.

VOSTOK 1	
LAUNCH	12 APRIL 1961
DURATION OF MISSION	108 MINUTES
SIZE	2.3-M-(7.5-FT) DIAMETER SPHERE + 2.25-M-(7.4-FT) LENGTH EQUIPMENT MODULE
MASS	4,730 KG (10,428 LB)

The module was controlled from the ground because no one knew how weightlessness would affect a human. However, a sealed envelope containing the code to the manual controls was provided in case of emergency.

THE 'LITTLE SPHERE'

Vostok consisited of two parts. One, nicknamed 'sharik' ('little sphere') was the crew and re-entry module in which Gagarin sat. The other was the equipment module that held the engines and fuel. At the end of the mission, the two separated, and the retro-engine on the equipment module fired the re-entry module towards Earth. There was no control over its path.

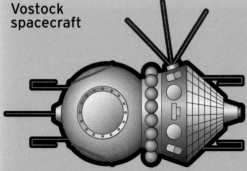

Vostock spacecraft

Re-entry module   Equipment module

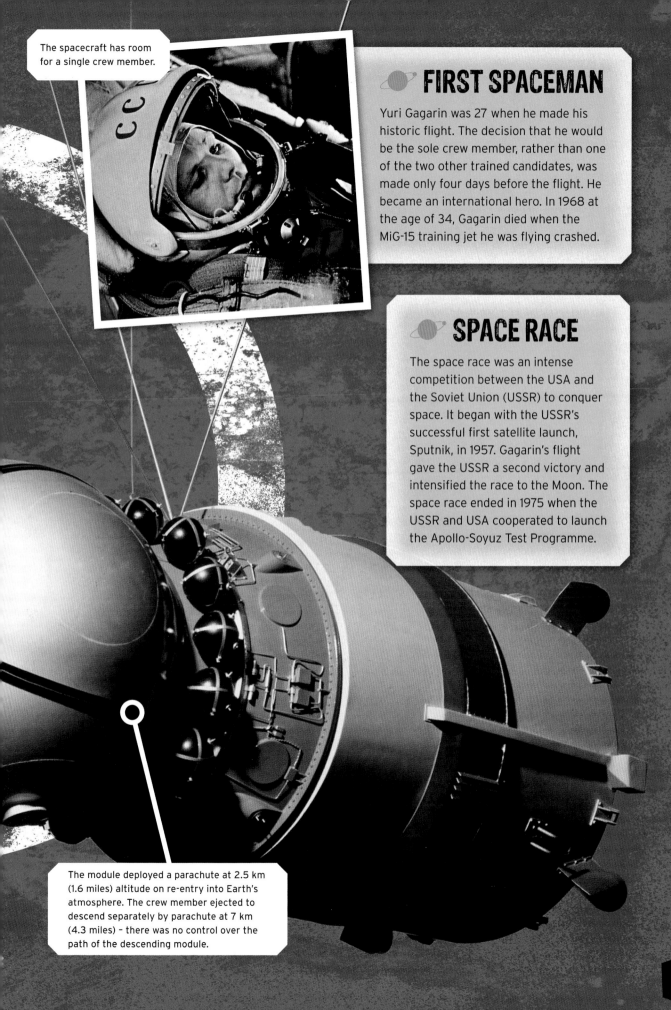

The spacecraft has room for a single crew member.

FIRST SPACEMAN

Yuri Gagarin was 27 when he made his historic flight. The decision that he would be the sole crew member, rather than one of the two other trained candidates, was made only four days before the flight. He became an international hero. In 1968 at the age of 34, Gagarin died when the MiG-15 training jet he was flying crashed.

SPACE RACE

The space race was an intense competition between the USA and the Soviet Union (USSR) to conquer space. It began with the USSR's successful first satellite launch, Sputnik, in 1957. Gagarin's flight gave the USSR a second victory and intensified the race to the Moon. The space race ended in 1975 when the USSR and USA cooperated to launch the Apollo-Soyuz Test Programme.

The module deployed a parachute at 2.5 km (1.6 miles) altitude on re-entry into Earth's atmosphere. The crew member ejected to descend separately by parachute at 7 km (4.3 miles) – there was no control over the path of the descending module.

FIRST ANIMAL IN SPACE

FRUIT FLIES

The very first animals to go into space were tiny fruit flies on 20 February 1947. They were packed into a Blossom space capsule and blasted to 109 km (68 miles) using a V-2 rocket.

The point of the experiment was to examine the effects of radiation at high altitude. The fruit flies were recovered alive after the trip, when the module parachuted safely to Earth. Later animals sent to space were not always so lucky.

At 2.5 mm (0.098 in) long, a fruit fly weighs just 1 mg (3.5 oz).

FIRST TEST PILOTS

Using animals to test flight has a long history. Joseph-Michel and Jacques-Étienne Mongolfier tested their new invention – a hot-air balloon – in France in 1783 by sending up a sheep, a duck and a rooster in one. The sheep was used as its body weight is comparable with a human's. The duck and rooster were controls, to reveal any ill effects from the aircraft rather than the altitude as they can fly anyway.

V-2 CARRYING FRUIT FLIES

DATE	20 FEBRUARY 1947
NATIONALITY	USA
ALTITUDE	109 KM (68 MILES)
DURATION	6 MINUTES, 59 SECONDS

TORTOISES IN SPACE

The first animals on a space flight to go beyond Earth's orbit were passengers on the Zond 5 spacecraft (USSR) launched 18 September 1968. Two tortoises, some wine flies and mealworms flew all around the Moon before landing safely back on Earth with a splashdown in the Indian Ocean. The first manned orbit of the Moon was 21 December 1968, in Apollo 8.

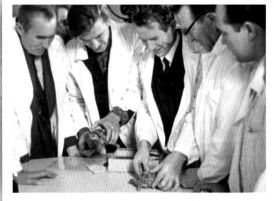

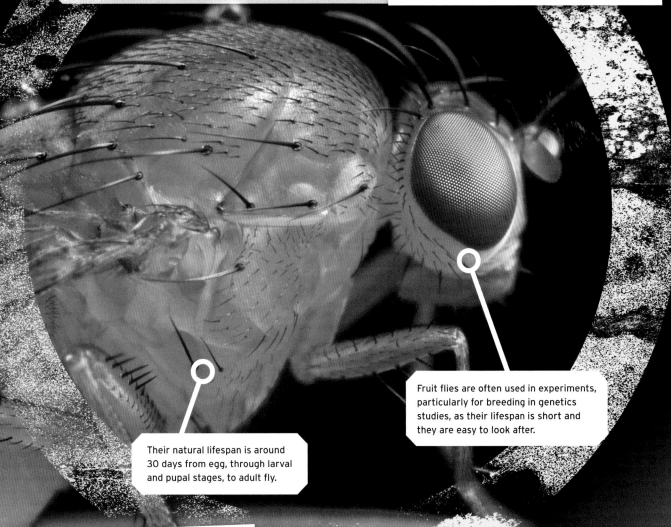

Fruit flies are often used in experiments, particularly for breeding in genetics studies, as their lifespan is short and they are easy to look after.

Their natural lifespan is around 30 days from egg, through larval and pupal stages, to adult fly.

PERILS OF SPACE FLIGHT

Early concerns about radiation — 'cosmic rays' — in low space flight were unfounded, but astronauts do suffer from 'space sickness' caused by weightlessness. Space sickness causes headaches and nausea or vomiting. It's worse in large spacecraft where there is room for astronauts to float around. Long periods in space have more serious effects, including muscles wasting away and bones losing density.

FIRST EARTH ORBIT

SPUTNIK

The satellite Sputnik, launched by the USSR on 4 October 1957, was the first human-made object to go into orbit around the Earth. Over a period of three months, it orbited Earth 1,350 times.

Launched by rocket, Sputnik blasted to an altitude of 223 km (139 miles) above the Earth. It went into a non-circular orbit, which had a lowest point ('perigee') of 223 km (139 miles) and a highest point ('apogee') of 950 km (590 miles). After three months, Sputnik burned up while re-entering Earth's atmosphere.

SPUTNIK

SIZE	58.5-CM (23-IN) DIAMETER
MASS	83.6 KG (184 LB)
LAUNCHED	4 OCTOBER 1957
DURATION OF MISSION	92 DAYS
ORBITS COMPLETED	1,350

Four aerials, each 5.3 m (17.4 ft) long, broadcast radio signals. The 'beep, beep' sound transmitted could be picked up by radio receivers all over Earth as Sputnik passed overhead.

WHAT'S THE USE?

Modern satellites have many uses, including mapping the Earth, conducting scientific studies of conditions on Earth and in space, tracking weather, telecommunications (mobile phones and satellite TV), spying (with cameras snooping on areas of land and sea), and navigation ('satnav'). Information travels to and from satellites at the speed of light – nearly 300,000 km (186,411 miles) per second – so there is no noticeable delay, even though your phone conversation has been bounced through space!

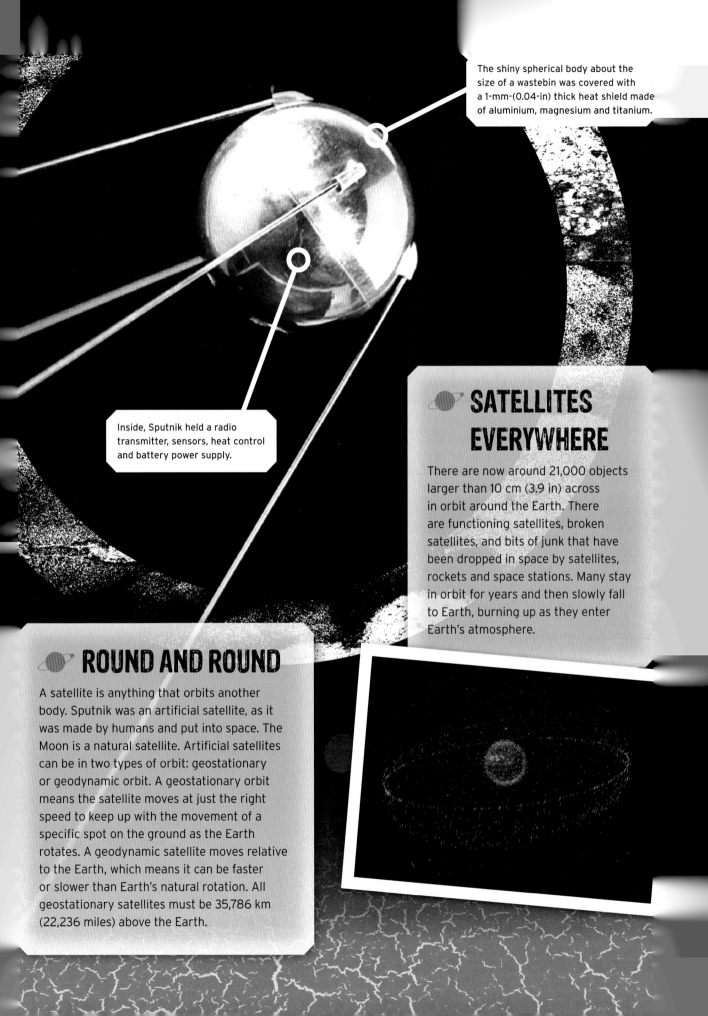

The shiny spherical body about the size of a wastebin was covered with a 1-mm-(0.04-in) thick heat shield made of aluminium, magnesium and titanium.

Inside, Sputnik held a radio transmitter, sensors, heat control and battery power supply.

🪐 SATELLITES EVERYWHERE

There are now around 21,000 objects larger than 10 cm (3.9 in) across in orbit around the Earth. There are functioning satellites, broken satellites, and bits of junk that have been dropped in space by satellites, rockets and space stations. Many stay in orbit for years and then slowly fall to Earth, burning up as they enter Earth's atmosphere.

🪐 ROUND AND ROUND

A satellite is anything that orbits another body. Sputnik was an artificial satellite, as it was made by humans and put into space. The Moon is a natural satellite. Artificial satellites can be in two types of orbit: geostationary or geodynamic orbit. A geostationary orbit means the satellite moves at just the right speed to keep up with the movement of a specific spot on the ground as the Earth rotates. A geodynamic satellite moves relative to the Earth, which means it can be faster or slower than Earth's natural rotation. All geostationary satellites must be 35,786 km (22,236 miles) above the Earth.

BEST LIGHT SHOW ON EARTH

THE NORTHERN LIGHTS

The Northern lights — or aurora borealis — light up the sky with brilliant swirls and bands of bright colours. They're seen near the North Pole, while the Southern lights — aurora australis — are seen near the South Pole.

The light is produced by highly charged electrons from space interacting with gas atoms in the atmosphere. Energy from the interaction is released as photons — parcels of light. The colour of the light emitted depends on whether the particles hit an oxygen or a nitrogen atom. Oxygen produces green or brownish-red light, and nitrogen produces red or blue.

Colours can swirl around constantly, changing in seconds, or remain much the same for hours on end.

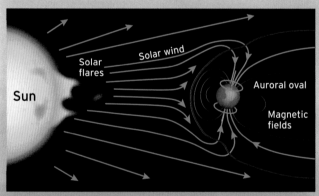

Solar flares

Solar wind

Sun

Auroral oval

Magnetic fields

HOW THE AURORA WORKS

The Sun pours out a constant stream of charged particles — electrons and protons — which sweep through the solar system. As they rush by, some are dragged off course by Earth's magnetic field and carried towards the poles where they collide with gas atoms in the upper atmosphere. Solar flares from the Sun send out extra charged particles, making dramatic aurorae on Earth a couple of days later.

🪐 ON OTHER PLANETS

Aurorae don't only exist on Earth. Any planet with a strong magnetosphere (where charged particles are controlled by an object's magnetic field) and some form of atmosphere can have aurorae near its poles. Aurorae have been spotted on Jupiter, Saturn, Uranus, Neptune and Mars.

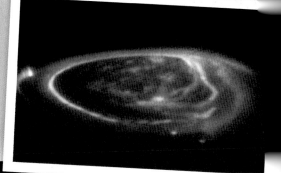

Green light is the most common colour; bright blue is the rarest colour.

🪐 WHEN AND WHERE TO WATCH

The aurorae are best seen near — but not at — the poles during times of sunspot activity (highly magnetic patches on the sun's surface) or solar flares. In the north, they are visible in Canada, northern Russia, Scandinavia, Iceland, Greenland and even Scotland. In the south, they are seen in Australia, New Zealand, South America and Antarctica. But the most amazing view of all is from space.

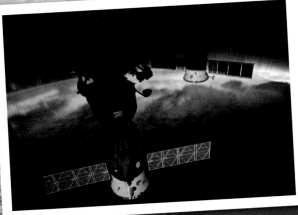

The lowest part of the aurora is about 100 km (62 miles) above the ground. The top can be over 300 km (186.4 miles). Green light is produced closer to Earth and red light higher up.

AURORA BOREALIS AND AURORA AUSTRALIS

FIRST NAMED	1621, BY PIERRE GASSENDI
WHERE SEEN	WITHIN 3° TO 6° OF LATITUDE OF THE NORTH AND SOUTH POLES

FIRST INTERPLANETARY PROBE

MARINER 2

The first spacecraft ever to fly past another planet was Mariner 2. Its flyby of Venus on 14 December 1962 marked the longest successful space flight at the time.

The flight to Venus took 109 days. On the way, Mariner 2 measured the solar wind and density of cosmic dust. Arriving at Venus, it calculated the temperature and mass of the planet. Mariner 2 sent data back to Earth until 3 January 1963, and is still orbiting the Sun.

The hexagonal hub contains electronic equipment for science experiments and a radio transmitter; the battery and charging unit; the rocket engine and altitude control. The radio dish antenna is attached to one end of the hub.

MARINER 2

LAUNCH DATE	27 AUGUST 1962
DURATION OF MISSION	129 DAYS
FURTHEST DISTANCE FROM EARTH	105,464,560 KM (65,532,639 MILES)
SIZE	5.05 M (16.6 FT) SPAN (ACROSS SOLAR WINGS); 3.66 M (12 FT) LENGTH

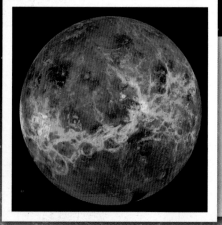

CRUSHING AND HOT

The temperature on Venus is close to 500 °C (932 °F), and the pressure is so high that spacecraft must be carefully constructed to avoid being crushed. The toxic atmosphere is a poisonous mix of carbon dioxide and nitrogen with clouds of sulphuric acid.

Two solar-cell wings collect energy from the Sun to power the craft and recharge the battery.

VENUS AND EARTH

Venus is the brightest star in our evening sky and sometimes the closest planet to Earth. Mercury, Venus and Mars all take different amounts of time to orbit the Sun, so the distance between them and Earth varies a lot. At its closest, Venus is 38 million km (23.6 million miles) away, and at its most distant it is 261 million km (just over 162 million miles) away. Venus rotates so slowly that a day on Venus is as long as 243 Earth days. But a year on Venus is 223 Earth days — its day is longer than its year!

A boom extending from the hub holds the scientific instruments for collecting data.

FAILURES AND SUCCESSES

Before Mariner 2, Mariner 1 was accidentally blown up at launch on 22 July 1962 after developing a fault. The USSR probe Venera 1, launched 12 February 1961, lost contact after seven days.

FIRST ROBOTIC ROVER

The lid had a solar panel on the underside, which collected power during the day. The lid closed at night while the rover was inactive.

LUNOKHOD 1

The first remote-controlled robotic rover on the Moon was Lunokhod 1, carried by Luna 17 launched from the USSR. It landed on the Moon on 17 November 1970.

Lunokhod had equipment to study the lunar surface and send data and photos back to Earth. It sent 20,000 images of the surface and analysed 25 soil samples. It worked during the lunar day and hibernated during the lunar night. A full lunar day is the equivalent of a month on Earth.

 ## SECRET MISSION

Lunokhod 1's mission was to search for possible landing sites on the Moon, and places where a lunar base might be established in the future. Intended to work for three lunar days, the rover actually operated for 11 Earth months. Lunokhod 1 is still on the Moon today — it was rediscovered by NASA in 2010.

The tub-shaped main body had eight wheels, each powered separately.

LUNOKHOD 1	
LAUNCH DATE	10 NOVEMBER 1970
LENGTH	2.3 M (7.5 FT)
MASS	756 KG (1,667 LB)
OPERATED FOR	322 DAYS
DISTANCE TRAVELLED	10.5 KM (6.5 MILES)

LIFE AFTER DEATH

Lunokhod 1 stopped transmitting data in 1971, but it's still useful. A team in the USA is using Lunokhod's reflector to help measure the distance between Earth and the Moon. The Lunar Laser Ranging experiment bounces laser beams off reflective surfaces on the Moon and measures the time it takes for the reflection to reach Earth. The team is aiming to calculate distances to an accuracy of 1 mm (0.04 in), and is the most accurate measurement of the Moon ever attempted.

A reflector was used to bounce laser light beamed from Earth. Measuring the time the reflection took to return to Earth gave exact information about the position of the rover and the Moon.

BACK TO THE MOON

After Lunokhod 1 and Lunokhod 2 (1973), no more robotic rovers were deployed until 1997, when the US rover Sojourner landed on Mars as part of the Pathfinder mission. The only robotic rover on the Moon since the Lunokhod missions has been the Chinese Jade Rabbit, which landed on 14 December 2013.

FIRST HUMAN ON THE MOON

FIRST MOON LANDING

The first human to set foot on ground beyond Earth was Neil Armstrong, who stepped on to the surface of the Moon at 02:56 (GMT, or UK time) on 21 July 1969. While doing so he activated TV cameras strapped to his spacesuit and said, "That's one small step for a man; one giant leap for mankind".

The Apollo 11 crew collected 21.5 kg (47 lb) of moon rock to bring back and installed instruments, including a seismometer to record moonquakes and a retroreflector to bounce laser beams from Earth and measure the distance between Earth and the Moon.

APOLLO 11 CREW

Apollo 11 was launched by a three-stage Saturn V rocket on 16 July 1969 with a crew of three: Neil Armstrong (commander, left), Michael Collins (centre) and Buzz Aldrin (right). Armstrong and Aldrin walked on the Moon, but Collins piloted the command module in orbit around the Moon.

Footprints left on the Moon could last forever as there is nothing to disturb them. They could easily still be there millions of years after humans are extinct.

HOW TO GET TO THE MOON

The first two rocket stages blasted the command and service modules into space, and the third put it in orbit around the Moon. Each stage fell away after use. The lunar excursion module separated to land on the Moon while the command module remained in orbit. The excursion module had its own rocket to leave the surface and rejoin the command module for the return to Earth.

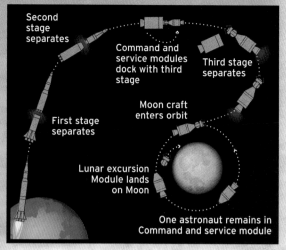

Second stage separates

First stage separates

Command and service modules dock with third stage

Third stage separates

Moon craft enters orbit

Lunar excursion Module lands on Moon

One astronaut remains in Command and service module

The US flag planted on the Moon had to be wired to look as if it were flying, as there is no wind on the Moon. It was knocked over by the blast from the engines of the lunar module taking off.

 # MORE MOON LANDINGS

There have been six manned Moon landings, all sent from the USA. The seventh attempt, Apollo 13, was aborted before reaching the Moon.

Two astronauts spent 21 hours and 31 minutes on the surface of the Moon. They were outside the lunar module for only 2.5 hours.

FIRST MOON LANDING

DATE	21 JULY 1969
ASTRONAUTS ON THE MOON	NEIL ARMSTRONG, BUZZ ALDRIN
TIME SPENT ON MOON	21 HOURS, 31 MINUTES
MISSION COMMANDER	NEIL ARMSTRONG
DURATION OF APOLLO 11 MISSION	8 DAYS, 3 HOURS, 18 MINUTES

FASTEST HUMAN SPACE FLIGHT

APOLLO 10

Apollo 10 reached a top speed of 39,897 km/h (24,791 mph) on its return to Earth on 26 May 1969.

The Apollo 10 mission was a practice run for the Apollo 11 Moon landing in July 1969. It was the fourth manned space flight in seven months. Apollo 10 went into orbit around the Moon, then the lunar module separated from the command and service module and descended to within 14 km (9 miles) of the Moon's surface, but did not land.

APOLLO 10

LAUNCH DATE:	18 MAY 1969
MISSION DURATION:	8 DAYS, 3 MINS
TOP SPEED:	39,897 KM/H (24,791 MPH)

The first stage of Saturn V blasted Apollo 10 from the launch pad with a force of 3.5 million kg (7.7 million lb).

 PRACTICE MAKES PERFECT

President John F Kennedy declared in 1961 that the USA would put a man on the Moon by the end of the 1960s. The Apollo programme was developed to make this happen.

The whole rocket was 110.6 m (363 ft) tall and weighed 2.7 million kg (6 million lb), with the Apollo craft accounting for less than a quarter of the length.

Mission	Launch Date	Purpose
Apollo 7	11 October 1968	Astronauts orbit Earth; first live TV broadcast from space
Apollo 8	21 December 1968	First astronauts to leave Earth orbit; first to orbit the Moon; first to see the far side of the Moon; first to see whole of Earth from space
Apollo 9	3 March 1969	First to dock and fly a lunar module; first spacewalk
Apollo 10	18 May 1969	Full test-run of everything except Moon landing

The command module, which returned to Earth reaching record-breaking speed, was carried on top of the Saturn V rocket.

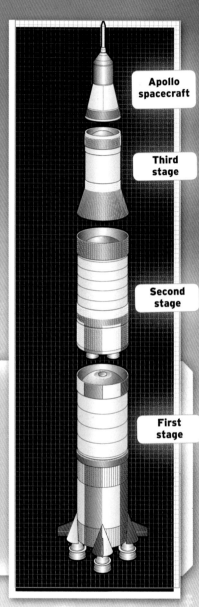

Apollo spacecraft

Third stage

Second stage

First stage

GOING UP...

All the manned Apollo missions launched on Saturn V rockets. The rocket had three stages, with the Apollo craft on the top. The rocket engines fired in turn and dropped away when their fuel was used up. The first stage blasted the craft off the launch pad. The second boosted it to a higher altitude. The third put it into Earth's orbit, then shut down. It fired again to send the craft into orbit around the Moon.

...AND COMING DOWN

The return journey takes less power and fuel because gravity pulls the craft towards Earth. Only the command and support modules remain for the return flight, using a hydrogen fuel cell for power. The support module separates and is slowed by a parachute as it descends before splashdown in the sea.

FIRST SPACE-WALK

LEONOV'S SPACEWALK

The first person ever to carry out a spacewalk was Russian cosmonaut Alexey Leonov on 18 March 1965. Leonov ventured outside his craft, Voskhod 2, for 12 minutes. He claimed he felt "like a seagull with its wings outstretched, soaring high above the Earth".

The spacewalk went smoothly until Leonov tried to re-enter the craft. He found his suit had become so distorted by air inside it expanding during the walk that it was impossible to manoeuvre through the hatch as planned. He had to release oxygen into space from his suit and go through the hatch head first, a difficult task that he only just managed.

 WHY WALK IN SPACE?

Leonov's spacewalk was intended to test whether a human being could survive in space outside a spacecraft. Since then, spacewalks have been carried out as part of experiments, and to maintain, mend and service spacecraft and satellites.

LEONOV'S SPACEWALK

DATE	18 MARCH 1965
DURATION	12 MINUTES, 9 SECONDS
MISSION	VOSKHOD 2

IN TROUBLE

Leonov's father watched the broadcast at his home with journalists present. Seeing his son's historic spacewalk, he shouted: "Why is he acting like a juvenile delinquent? Everyone else can complete their mission properly, inside the spacecraft. What is he doing clambering about outside? Somebody must tell him to get back inside immediately. He must be punished for this". Thanks, Dad!

SPORTS IN SPACE

In 2013, Russian cosmonauts took the Olympic torch for a spacewalk. It was the first time the Olympic torch had been outside Earth's atmosphere, but of course it couldn't burn in space. Usually, the torch is lit in Greece and the flame is carried around the world to the site of the next Olympic Games, arriving for the opening ceremony.

A 5.35-m (17.5-ft) tether attached to Voskhod 2 prevented Leonov drifting away into space.

In the report Leonov wrote after his mission, the cosmonaut stated that "provided with a special suit, man can work and survive in open space. Thank you for your attention".

Leonov's spacesuit had nine of aluminium foil as well as and hard layers. The suit ne keep the cosmonaut warm i sub-zero temperatures of s

FIRST UNTETHERED SPACEWALK

JET-POWERED BACKPACK

Leonov remained connected to his spacecraft during his spacewalk. The first astronaut to move untethered — freely — through space was American Bruce McCandless II on 7 February 1984.

To control his movement in space, McCandless used a jet-powered backpack that he had helped design. His first unconnected spacewalk, from the space shuttle Challenger, lasted just over an hour. It was the first part of an EV (extra-vehicular) mission of 5 hours 55 minutes shared between two astronauts. McCandless travelled about 100 m (328 ft) from Challenger.

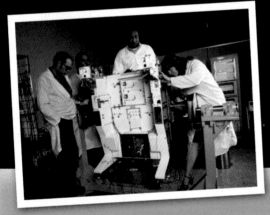

The astronaut controls speed and direction of travel using hand controls on the MMU: the left-hand controller for up, down, left, right, forward and backwards, and the right-hand controller to rotate.

🪐 HANDS-FREE

The MMU (Manned Maneuvering Unit) made untethered spacewalks possible. It was powered by liquid nitrogen, which the astronaut could release in bursts from any combination of 24 nozzles. The force of the nitrogen leaving the nozzle pushed the astronaut forward through space. The astronaut used hand controls to change the direction of travel. They could also be locked in position so the astronaut's hands were free for work.

On a spacewalk, an astronaut is so high up that he or she is not pulled back to Earth by gravity.

The MMU is worn as a backpack and replaces the tether used on earlier spacewalks.

🪐 LONGEST SPACEWALK

The longest-ever spacewalk lasted 8 hours and 56 minutes on 11 March 2001. It was carried out by Susan Helms and James Voss on a space shuttle mission to the International Space Station (ISS). They made changes to the configuration of the space station during their spacewalk.

UNTETHERED SPACEWALK MISSION, STS-41B EV1

PERFORMED BY	BRUCE McCANDLESS II
DATE	7 FEBRUARY 1984
DURATION	1 HR (OF 5 HRS 55 MINS TOTAL EV MISSION)
DISTANCE TRAVELLED	100 M (328 FT)
ALTITUDE	278 KM (173 MILES)

Control and display panel

Helmet lights

Emergency O2 hose

🪐 SUITED TO SPACE

The MMU fits over the astronaut's spacesuit, which keeps him or her alive in space. It protects against the low pressure and freezing temperatures in space and provides the astronaut with oxygen. Without a spacesuit, an astronaut would swell and lose consciousness in 15 seconds and would eventually freeze or explode. The design of spacesuits is still evolving today.

LONGEST STAY IN SPACE

MIR SPACE STATION

Russian cosmonaut Valeri Polyakov spent the whole of 1994 and the first months of 1995 on the space station Mir, completing the longest ever space flight of 437 days.

This record-breaking trip was Polyakov's second tour in space. The first lasted 240 days from 28 August 1988 to 28 April 1989. Until 1999 he held the record for the total number of days spent in space, with 678 days over both missions. That record is now held by Sergei Krikalev with 803 days over six missions from 1988 to 2005.

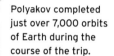

Polyakov completed just over 7,000 orbits of Earth during the course of the trip.

MAN ON A MISSION

Polyakov's mission was to test the effects of a very long space flight, part of the research into whether a flight to Mars would be possible. He suffered no lasting bad effects, but reported a decline in mood — feeling more miserable — during the first weeks in space and after returning to Earth. After landing on Earth, he walked a short distance from the capsule to a chair to show that an astronaut would be fit to move when arriving on Mars. Long spaceflights damage human bones and muscles, so it was important to see how fit an astronaut would be after the flight.

POLYAKOV'S STAY IN MIR, 1994–95

DATE	8 JANUARY 1994 – 22 MARCH 1995
DURATION	437 DAYS 18 HRS
DISTANCE TRAVELLED	291 MILLION KM (180 MILLION MILES)
TIME-DILATION EFFECT	0.017 SECONDS

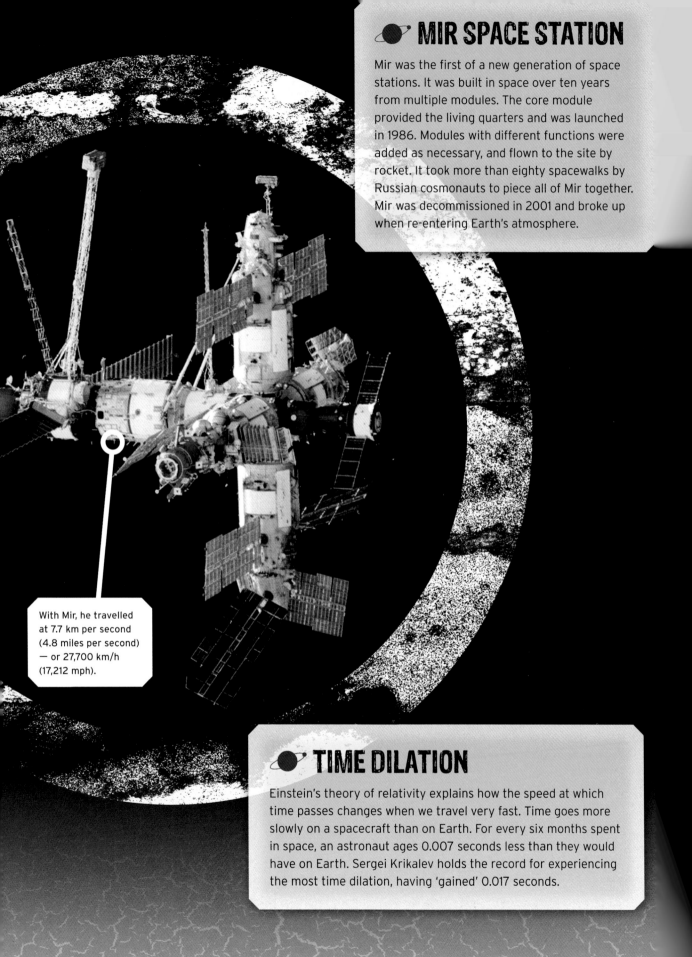

🪐 MIR SPACE STATION

Mir was the first of a new generation of space stations. It was built in space over ten years from multiple modules. The core module provided the living quarters and was launched in 1986. Modules with different functions were added as necessary, and flown to the site by rocket. It took more than eighty spacewalks by Russian cosmonauts to piece all of Mir together. Mir was decommissioned in 2001 and broke up when re-entering Earth's atmosphere.

With Mir, he travelled at 7.7 km per second (4.8 miles per second) — or 27,700 km/h (17,212 mph).

🪐 TIME DILATION

Einstein's theory of relativity explains how the speed at which time passes changes when we travel very fast. Time goes more slowly on a spacecraft than on Earth. For every six months spent in space, an astronaut ages 0.007 seconds less than they would have on Earth. Sergei Krikalev holds the record for experiencing the most time dilation, having 'gained' 0.017 seconds.

SMALLEST PLANET

The surface temperature is either scorching hot or freezing cold.

MERCURY

Mercury, the planet closest to the Sun, is also the smallest planet in the solar system. It's slightly larger than Earth's moon and smaller than the moons Ganymede (of Jupiter) and Titan (of Saturn).

Although it's small, Mercury is fierce. There is no atmosphere to protect it from wildly swinging temperatures. The part of the planet facing the Sun can reach a temperature of 427 °C (800.6 °F), while on the side in darkness the temperature can drop to -173 °C (-279.4 °F).

Mercury turns on its own axis so slowly that it has only three days spread over two of its years.

Craters up to 25 km (15.5 miles) across have been left by impacts from meteors and asteroids, as well as by volcanic eruptions millions of years ago, or billions of years ago when the planet was forming.

 EXOSPHERE

Mercury doesn't have an atmosphere, but it does have an exosphere. This is a layer of gas so thin that it doesn't exert any significant pressure. The molecules of gas escape from the rocks on the surface and are held near the planet by gravity. Earth's moon also has an exosphere. On even smaller moons and asteroids, gas molecules escape straight into space as there is not enough gravity to hold them captive.

MERCURY

DISTANCE FROM SUN	58 MILLION KM (0.39 AU) (36 MILLION MILES)
ROTATIONAL TIME (LENGTH OF DAY)	59 EARTH DAYS
ORBITAL TIME (LENGTH OF YEAR)	88 EARTH DAYS
MASS	3.3×10^{23} KG (= 0.055 X EARTH) (7.3×10^{23} LB)
DIAMETER	4,879 KM (= 0.38 X EARTH) (3.03 MILES)

IRON SNOW

Mercury has a hard surface. The planet is made of metal (70%) and rock (30%), making it dense for its size. The hard crust is pitted and scarred by meteorite impacts. Mercury's core is huge — it accounts for 85% of the planet's diameter. The core is probably a mix of liquid iron and sulphur. As the iron cools, it falls in tiny fragments, rather like snowflakes, which drift slowly towards the very centre of the planet, the deepest part of the core.

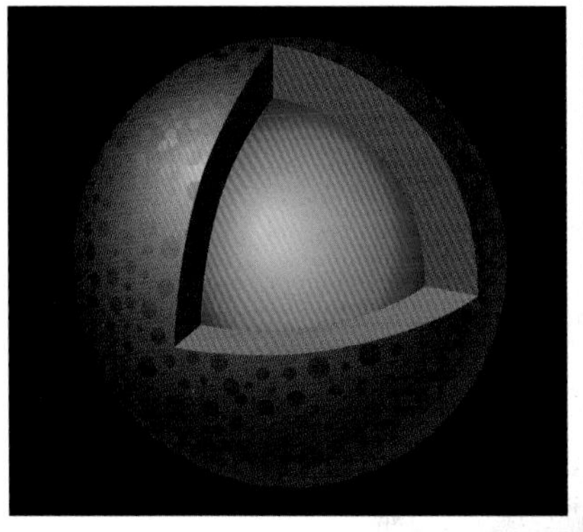

MISSIONS TO MERCURY

Mercury is hard to visit as it's so close to the Sun. Two probes have explored Mercury so far. Mariner 10, launched in 1973, photographed half the surface during three fly-bys. Messenger (shown here), launched in 2004, went into orbit around Mercury in 2011. Its mission is to map the surface and measure data, revealing the internal structure and magnetosphere.

DENSEST THING

BLACK HOLES

The densest known thing in the universe is a black hole. Its gravity is so extreme it drags in all nearby matter and even energy, crushing them under immense pressure.

A black hole is an area of super-compressed matter that is infinitely small. It can be created when a star dies. If the star starts at about 20 times the mass of our sun, it eventually collapses in on itself. Its gravity increases as it does so, pulling itself into a smaller and smaller space, becoming ever more dense. The more massive stars become black holes. Many — perhaps all — galaxies have massive black holes at their centre.

The boundary around a black hole marking the point of no return is called the event horizon. Nothing can escape from within the event horizon. The diameter of the event horizon is determined by the mass of the black hole.

BIG AND SMALL

The smallest black holes might have an event horizon the size of a single atom, yet they have the mass of a mountain. These might have been created when the universe first formed. Larger black holes, called stellar black holes, have twenty times the mass of our sun. Super-massive black holes can have as much mass as a million suns and are found at the centres of galaxies. The largest of all, ultra-massive black holes, might have the mass of 40 billion suns.

ULTRA-MASSIVE BLACK HOLES

MASS	40 BILLION TIMES OUR SUN
DISTANCE FROM EARTH	13 BILLION LIGHT YEARS

hole as its gravity is too strong for anything to escape — even light.

NEUTRON STARS

Neutron stars are the densest objects we can observe directly as they can still emit radiation. A neutron star is the core left behind after a star has exploded as a supernova. It can be about 20 km (12.4 miles) across, but still has the mass of a star. Even more dense is a special type of neutron star with an extremely powerful magnetic field, called a magnetar. A teaspoon of magnetar would have a mass of about 100 billion tonnes (110 billion tons). A neutron star can spin extremely fast — as fast as the blades of a kitchen blender, or 43,000 times a minute.

THE HOLE IN THE MIDDLE

Astronomers believe there is a super-massive black hole at the centre of every large galaxy. The one at the centre of our galaxy, the Milky Way, is in a region called Sagittarius A*. Luckily for you and me, the Earth is not in danger of being sucked into it — it's 26,000 light years away.

The effects on nearby matter are the give-away signs that a black hole is present — it can't be observed directly.

FIRST MAMMAL IN SPACE

ALBERT II'S FLIGHT

A rhesus monkey called Albert II was the first mammal to go into space on 14 June 1949.

Albert was seated in a V-2 Blossom rocket, which blasted to a height of 134 km (83 miles). The aim of the mission, as with other early missions that sent animals into space, was to investigate the effects of space travel and acceleration on the body before humans ventured into space. Unfortunately, a problem with the parachute used for the capsule on re-entry led to Albert's death at the end of the flight.

Albert was anaesthetized during the flight. Electrodes monitored his condition constantly.

THERE AND BACK AGAIN

The first monkeys to go successfully into space and survive were Miss Baker and Able, on 28 May 1959. They achieved an altitude of 579 km (360 miles). Sadly, Able died on 1 June 1959 because of an unusual reaction to an anaesthetic during an operation, but Miss Baker lived to the age of 27. Her 20th birthday was marked with balloons and a party, and she lived as a celebrity for the rest of her life.

An earlier attempt to launch a monkey into space, Albert I, was unsuccessful. It did not go high enough to count as reaching space.

SPACE MONKEYS

The USA sent a total of 32 monkeys into space. One of the most important was Ham, the first chimpanzee in space. His flight on 31 January 1961 reached 252.5 km (157 miles) and a speed of 9,426 km/h (5,857 mph). Ham was not just a passenger, as previous monkeys had been. He was trained to operate levers in the craft. The flight lasted 16 minutes and 30 seconds. His healthy return paved the way for manned space flights. Just three months later, Alan Shepard became the first American astronaut in space.

ALBERT II'S FLIGHT

DATE	14 JUNE 1949
ALTITUDE	134 KM (83 MILES)

Albert II was constrained in a small, rigid capsule to prevent him moving or tumbling around during the flight.

TIMES CHANGE

When animals are sent into space these days, much more attention is paid to their welfare. They are properly looked after, and every effort is made to make sure they get back to Earth safely and are comfortable on their flight. There is still a lot we can learn about how living things adapt to cope in space, which will help with longer space missions.

PLANET WITH MOST MOONS

JUPITER

While Earth has only one moon, and some planets have none at all, Jupiter holds the record for the largest number of moons with 67.

Jupiter was the first planet found to have moons besides Earth. The four largest moons, known as the Galilean moons, were discovered by Galileo in 1610. In addition, Jupiter has four other regular satellites that orbit close to the planet and many much smaller moons, some far away.

JUPITER	
MOONS	67
RINGS	3
MASS	1.9 X 10^{27} KG (4.2 X 10^{27} LB) (318 X EARTH)
DIAMETER	71,500 KM (44,428 MILES) (11 X EARTH)
DISTANCE FROM SUN	5.2 AU
LENGTH OF DAY	ALMOST 10 HOURS
ORBITAL PERIOD (YEAR)	4,333 DAYS (11 YRS, 318 DAYS)

 ## THE BIG FOUR

The Galilean moons, large enough for Galileo to have seen with his 30x magnification telescope, are the biggest moons in the solar system. These and the four other regular satellites are formed from Jupiter's own material. It's likely that earlier moons fell into Jupiter, throwing out new ones from the debris of the collision. The innermost moons, and unseen smaller moonlets, maintain Jupiter's rings by supplying them with dust.

MORE MOONS

The outer moons, many of them only a few kilometres (over a mile) across, have probably been captured by Jupiter. Scientists think they were passing material that was dragged into orbit by Jupiter's gravitational field. There is a space of 9 million km (5.6 million miles) between the Galilean moons and the outer moons, with only one moon — Thermista — in between.

A gas giant with no solid surface, Jupiter has three rings formed of dust and small particles of rock.

GASSY GIANT

Jupiter is a gas giant, the largest planet in the solar system. It has no solid surface, but a thick layer of atmosphere made of mostly hydrogen (90%) and helium, which lies around a core the size of Earth. The atmosphere is gas at the top, becoming liquid under pressure closer to the centre of the planet, so that there is an ocean of liquid, metallic hydrogen around the core. The core is probably a mix of metal and various forms of ice.

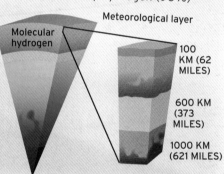

Molecular hydrogen

Meteorological layer

100 KM (62 MILES)

600 KM (373 MILES)

1000 KM (621 MILES)

Io is highly volcanically active, with a sea of hot, molten rock beneath a surface that looks like a cheesy pizza with tomato sauce.

The four largest moons are big enough to be considered dwarf planets if they were not satellites of another planet.

FURTHEST SPACECRAFT

VOYAGER 1

Voyager 1, launched in 1977, has travelled further than any other spacecraft and is now the most remote human-made object, over 21 billion km (13 billion miles) away.

Voyager 1 and its sister-craft Voyager 2 were sent on a mission to fly past and send data from the outer planets in the solar system and then head off into interstellar space. It took 36 years for Voyager 1 to reach the edge of the solar system, passing Saturn and Jupiter. It takes more than 17 hours for a radio signal to reach Earth from Voyager 1.

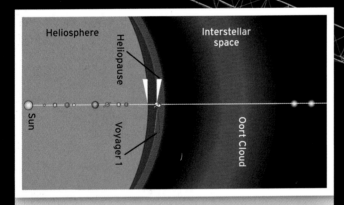

Heliosphere

Heliopause

Interstellar space

Sun

Voyager 1

Oort Cloud

🪐 WHERE NEXT?

As Voyager 1 leaves the solar system (above) it will head in the direction of the star Gliese 445. This star is currently approaching the solar system at 430,000 km/h (267,190 mph). After 40,000 years, Voyager 1 will pass within 1.6 light years of Gliese 445. The spacecraft will be powered until 2025, when Voyager will no longer have enough power to run its instruments. It will continue to move through space, though, until something destroys it. It may outlast humankind.

The Voyagers are powered by radioactive decay of plutonium oxide, which has a half-life of 87.7 years.

HOME OF COMETS

In 300 years, Voyager 1 will enter the Oort Cloud, a broad spherical region of ice and rock surrounding the solar system. The Oort Cloud probably contains billions of comets, some in a distant orbit and many we never see on Earth. It will take Voyager 1 about 30,000 years to pass through the Oort Cloud.

A giant radio antenna and receiving dish take up most of the bulk — this is how Voyager communicates with mission control on Earth.

VOYAGER 1

LAUNCH DATE	5 SEPTEMBER 1977
DISTANCE FROM EARTH	21 BILLION KM (13 BILLION MILES) (142 AU)
MASS	722 KG (1,592 LB)
VELOCITY	13 KM/SECOND (8 MILES/SECOND); 46,800 KM/H (29,080 MPH)

Only the size of a car, Voyager 1 is hurtling into interstellar space at 46,800 km/h (29,080 mph).

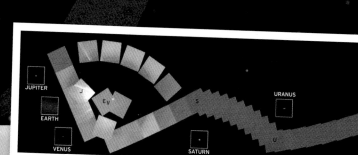

FAMILY PHOTO

Voyager has taken the most distant photo of Earth ever returned, which is included in the solar system 'family portrait' photo. This portrait was put together from photos taken by Voyager 1 on 14 February 1990. The image of Earth was taken at a distance of 6 billion km (3.7 billion miles).

MOST FAMOUS COMET

HALLEY'S COMET

The most famous comet is one that has been very important in the history of astronomy.

Edmond Halley figured out what comets are and how they work in 1705, by studying sightings of the comet which is now named after him. It's visible from Earth every 75 years, so most people get a chance to see it once in their lifetime.

HALLEY'S COMET

FIRST RECORDED	466–467 BC, Ancient Greece
RETURN PERIOD	75-76 years
LAST SEEN:	1986
NEXT DUE:	2061
DIMENSIONS:	15 x 8 x 8 km (9.3 x 5 x 5 miles)

The comet's surface has hills, mountains, ridges, dips and at least one crater, which was photographed by the probe Giotto in 1986.

🪐 COMETS

Comets are small balls of rock, dust and ice that orbit the sun on a non-circular orbit. When they are close enough to Earth to be visible, they appear as a bright spot followed by a streaming tail. The tail is made of matter 'outgassing' from the comet into space as it is heated by the sun. When Halley's comet passed Earth in 1910 it could be photographed for the first time — photography was only just being invented when it visited before!

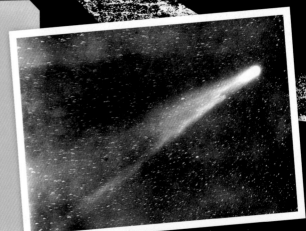

HALLEY'S DISCOVERY

The astronomer Edmond Halley proposed in 1705 that comets recorded in 1456, 1531, 1607 and 1682 were the same comet and that it would be seen again in 1758. Although Halley did not live to see the comet's return, he was right, and it became known as Halley's comet.

The comet's nucleus is made of rock particles, dust and ice and forms a 15-km (9.3 miles) long 'rubble pile' structure that looks like a peanut.

BAD LUCK

Comets have been noticed since prehistoric times. Before people knew that were space objects orbiting the Sun, many were afraid of comets, or saw them as omens indicating that something bad (or occasionally good) was about to happen. The Bayeux Tapestry, made to mark the victory of the French over the English at the Battle of Hastings in 1066, shows a comet that is likely to be Halley's comet.

COMING AND GOING

The nucleus of a comet can be from a few hundred metres to tens of kilometres across. Short-period comets are those with an orbit of less than 200 years; the shortest is Encke, at just over three years. Long-period comets, which go much further from the Sun, could have orbits up to millions of years. The longest known is Comet West at about 250,000 years.

The tail of gas and dust is up to 100 million km (62 million miles) long and 100,000 km (62,137 miles) across.

LARGEST SPACECRAFT

INTERNATIONAL SPACE STATION

The largest spacecraft ever built is the International Space Station (ISS), which is maintained by an international treaty and five space organizations representing the USA, Russia, Canada, Europe and Japan. It has been in low orbit over the Earth since 1998.

It is the base for experiments in many fields of science and has been visited by astronauts from 15 nations. ISS has been constantly occupied since 2 November 2000, making it the spacecraft with the longest-ever continuous occupation. It also holds the record as the single most expensive structure ever built, at $100 billion.

Eight pairs of 'sails' collect energy from the Sun to provide power.

BUILDING THE ISS

The first components were launched into space in November 1998 by Russian spacecraft. Other elements have been added since in stages, with the first crew arriving in 2000. Parts are fitted together robotically and by astronauts over a total of more than 1,000 hours of spacewalks.

LIFE ON BOARD

Crew sleep in either the American or the Russian quarters. Each crew member uses a tethered sleeping bag — if it's not attached to something, it floats freely around the spacecraft because of the lack of gravity. Most food is vacuum-packed in plastic bags. Because the sense of taste is reduced in space, astronauts use a lot of spice to make their food tasty. Any dropped crumbs have to be chased and caught so that they don't damage sensitive equipment or clog filters.

The ISS can be seen from Earth with the naked eye as a bright spot (illuminated by the Sun).

The ISS completes 15.5 orbits of the Earth each day. Altitude is maintained and altered by boosts from the engine of the Zvezda module and visiting spacecraft.

A DAY IN SPACE

Astronauts are usually woken at 06:00 and check the space station. Then they have breakfast and hold a daily planning conference with mission control. They start work at around 08:10. The day consists of work and exercise sessions, with a one-hour lunch break at 13:05. They stop work at 19:30, when they have dinner and a crew conference. The day ends at 21:30. They work ten hours each weekday, and five hours on Saturdays.

INTERNATIONAL SPACE STATION

LAUNCHED	1998 (FIRST COMPONENTS)
MASS	450,000 KG (99,2080 LB)
SPEED	27,600 KM/H (17,150 MPH)
ALTITUDE	330-435 KM (205-270 MILES)
SIZE	72.8 X 108.5 X 20 M (239 X 356 X 66 FT)

FIRST WOMAN IN SPACE

VALENTINA TERESHKOVA

The first woman in space was the Soviet cosmonaut Valentina Tereshkova, who went into space on Vostok 6 in 1963. She was also the first civilian in space.

Her mission was to gather data about the effects of space on the female body. She spent almost three days in space, orbiting the Earth 48 times. Her flight was longer than the total number of hours spent in space by all American astronauts at that time. Her daughter Elena, born in 1964, was the first person to have two parents who had both been into space. Her father, Andrian Nikolayev, was the third Russian cosmonaut.

 ## MISSION

Tereshkova was the only crew member of Vostok 6. She was sealed into the capsule two hours before take-off and spent a further 2 days and 52 hours strapped into a reclining seat in the craft. She took photographs and kept a detailed flight log, also recording her own physical condition. The capsule landed overland near a farm, narrowly missing a lake when she parachuted free.

The Vostok module was spherical, similar to that used by Yuri Gagarin for the first-ever manned space flight.

VALENTINA TERESHKOVA IN VOSTOK 6

LAUNCH DATE	16 JUNE 1963
CRAFT	VOSTOK 6 (USSR)
DURATION OF MISSION	2 DAYS, 22 HRS, 51 MINS
ALTITUDE	231 KM (143.5 MILES) (MAX)

🪐 BACKGROUND

Unlike most astronauts and cosmonauts, Tereshkova was not a pilot or aerospace engineer. She worked in a textile factory, and was selected for training because she was a keen amateur parachutist. Her father was a tractor driver and her mother a textile worker, and her family's humble background appealed to the Soviet government who celebrated the working class.

There was a single observation window for taking photos during the flight.

🪐 MORE WOMEN IN SPACE

It was 19 years after Tereshkova's flight before another woman went into space, the Russian cosmonaut Svetlana Savitskaya. During the twentieth anniversary of Tereshkova's flight, the first female US astronaut, Sally Ride, took off in the space shuttle Challenger. On 16 June 2012, the 49th anniversary of the launch of Vostok 6, Liu Yang became the first Chinese female astronaut (or 'taikonaut').

NEXT NEAREST STAR

PROXIMA CENTAURI

Our nearest star is the Sun but the next nearest star is Proxima Centauri in the constellation of Centaurus.

Although it's close in astronomical terms, Proxima Centauri is 4.2 light years from Earth, which means that the light we see now from Proxima Centauri left the star four years and three months ago. A spaceship like Voyager 1 would take more than 73,000 years to reach Proxima Centauri. Even a proposed nuclear-pulse-powered ship would take over 100 years.

Proxima Centauri shines with a reddish light, revealing that it's a red dwarf star.

PROXIMA CENTAURI

DISTANCE FROM EARTH	4.22 LIGHT YEARS
DISCOVERED	1915, BY ROBERT INNES
SIZE	195,000-KM (121,167-MILES) WIDTH ($\frac{1}{7}$ SUN'S RADIUS); WEIGHT ABOUT $\frac{1}{8}$ OUR SUN'S MASS
ROTATION PERIOD	83.5 DAYS
AGE	4.85 BILLION (4,850 MILLION)
REMAINING LIFE	4 TRILLION (4,000,000 MILLION) YEARS

RED DWARF

Proxima Centauri is a red dwarf — a small star emitting light at the red end of the visible spectrum. Our sun is a yellow dwarf. The star changes hydrogen into helium through nuclear fusion. As the hydrogen is used up, Proxima Centauri will get hotter and smaller. Its colour will change from red to blue and then white as it becomes a white dwarf — the last stage in its life as a star.

🪐 COMPANION STARS

Proxima Centauri is very close to the two stars of the Alpha Centauri group, Alpha Centauri A and B. These stars are much larger and brighter than Proxima Centauri, and only 0.21 light years away from it. It's likely that Proxima Centauri is part of the group, and might orbit Alpha Centauri with an orbital period of around half a million years.

The surface temperature is around 3,000 °C (5432 °F) — cooler than our Sun's 5,500°C (9932 °F).

🪐 COULD THERE BE LIFE?

There is no evidence of a habitable planet orbiting Proxima Centauri, but it's not impossible. Any planet would need to be close to its sun, with a 'year' of two Earth weeks or less. It would probably have its day and year 'locked' so that the same side of the planet always faced the sun, putting one side in permanent day and one in permanent night.

Only a seventh the width of our Sun, Proxima Centauri is not visible to the naked eye. It's so faint, that it would even be hard to see from one of its neighbouring stars.

LARGEST ICE GIANT

URANUS

The planet Uranus is a huge ice-giant — a mostly frozen ball, surrounded by a thick swirling atmosphere.

Uranus is the seventh planet from the Sun, and is much colder than the other gas giants, reaching a lowest temperature of -224.2 °C (-371.56 °F). It's windy, too, with storm winds reaching up to 900 km/h (559 mph).

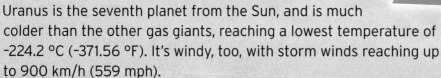

STRUCTURE OF URANUS

Uranus probably has a solid rocky core, about the size of Earth, surrounded by a mantle of ice, made of mixed water, ammonia and methane. Uranus has no solid surface, so there's no clear barrier between the mantle and the atmosphere. For convenience the 'surface' is considered the point at which the pressure is 1 bar (the same as sea-level atmospheric pressure on Earth). The atmosphere extends 50,000 km (31,069 miles) above the 'surface' — Earth's atmosphere is only 480 km (298 miles).

The atmosphere comprises 83% hydrogen, 15% helium and 2% methane in layers.

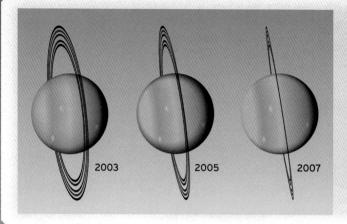

2003 2005 2007

 # LYING SIDEWAYS

It's hard to decide which is the north pole of Uranus as the planet lies almost exactly on its side. Its axis of rotation points towards the Sun — it spins so that first the north pole, then the south pole, faces the Sun each day. If Uranus turns in the same direction as Earth, it's tipped over a little more than 90 degrees; if its rotation is the other way (retrograde), like Venus, it's tilted a little less than 90 degrees.

The planet looks blue because methane in the upper atmosphere absorbs red light and reflects blue.

URANUS

DISTANCE FROM SUN	2.9 BILLION KM (1.8 BILLION MILES) (19.19 AU)
ROTATIONAL TIME (LENGTH OF DAY)	17 HOURS 14 MINUTES
ORBITAL TIME (LENGTH OF YEAR)	84 YEARS
MASS	8.7×10^{25} KG (14.5 X EARTH)
DIAMETER	50,720 KM (31,516 MILES) (OR 150,000 KM (93,206 MILES) INCLUDING ATMOSPHERE) (4 X EARTH)
MOONS	27 KNOWN
DATE OF DISCOVERY	1871
VISITED BY	VOYAGER 2, 24 JANUARY 1986

 # HOT ICE

Although the mantle of Uranus is called ice, it is a thick, fluid sludge of water, methane and ammonia, and isn't cold. The immense pressure, 100,000 times stronger than on Earth, forces chemicals that we usually find as liquids and gases to exist as solids and liquids.

Uranus has bands that show wind or storm systems in the atmosphere. These are not as easy to see as the bands on Jupiter and Saturn.

FIRST LANDING ON ANOTHER PLANET'S MOON

HUYGENS MISSION

When Huygens landed on Titan in 2005, it became the first spacecraft to land on the moon of a planet other than Earth.

The spacecraft Huygens was named after the Dutch astronomer Christiaan Huygens who discovered Saturn's moon Titan in 1655. Huygens was carried to Titan by the European Space Agency craft Cassini. After separating from Cassini, it spent 22 days drifting towards Titan. The descent through the atmosphere took 2 hours, and then Titan broadcast findings from the surface for 90 minutes.

Huygens was equipped for landing on either solid ground or in the ocean because no one knew what the landing site would be like.

TITAN

Titan is Saturn's largest moon, at 5,150 km (3,200 miles) across. Titan looks like a fuzzy orange ball, as its outline is blurred by a layer of methane gas 18-20-km (11-12.4-miles) thick. Methane is the gas we use for heating and cooking on Earth. In the northern part of the moon lies Kraken Mare, a vast lake of liquid hydrocarbons (chemicals made of carbon and hydrogen). Its surface has fields of dunes made of piled up fragments of hydrocarbons that have solidified from the atmosphere.

HUYGENS MISSION

CASSINI LAUNCH FROM EARTH	15 OCTOBER 1997
HUYGENS LAUNCH FROM CASSINI	25 DECEMBER 2004
LANDED ON TITAN	14 JANUARY 2005
DIAMETER	2.7 M (8.9 FT)
MASS	320 KG (705.5 LB)
DURATION	90 MINUTES

Huygens parachuted to the surface, sending data about the atmosphere to Earth.

🪐 CASSINI-HUYGENS

Cassini took seven years to reach Saturn. On the long journey, Huygens was in hibernation, only woken occasionally for tests. On the way, Cassini studied cosmic dust coming from Jupiter and from Saturn's rings. The particles of dust were a thousandth of a millimetre across — some even smaller — and travelling at up to 400 km (249 miles) per second.

The landing site had a surface of orange dust and scattered pebbles, which might have been little lumps of water ice.

🪐 HUYGENS ON TITAN

Huygens measured atmospheric conditions, wind speed and the gases found in the atmosphere as it descended towards Titan's surface. On landing, it bounced, slid and wobbled on the surface, which seemed to have a thin crust over something squashy or wet. The images from Huygens showed that the surface has been shaped by flowing liquid at some point.

MOST RECENTLY SEEN SUPERNOVA

SN1604

The last supernova seen with the naked eye in the Milky Way is called SN1604. It was witnessed by the great German astronomer Johannes Kepler in 1604.

At its brightest, the supernova was brighter than any other star in the sky (but the planet Venus is brighter). Although it's the most recently seen, the supernova event of SN1604 was actually longer ago than the first recorded supernova, but because it is so distant it took longer for the light to reach Earth.

The remnant of SN1604 is 14 light years across — 1.3×10^{17} km (0.8×10^{17} miles) wide.

SN1604

OBSERVED	1604
DISTANCE FROM EARTH	13,000-20,000 LIGHT YEARS AWAY

🪐 FIRST RECORDED SUPERNOVA

The first record of a supernova was made in AD 185. It was recorded by Chinese astronomers, who reported that it shone for around eight months. SN185, as it is now called, was a very large explosion — it seems a white dwarf sucked in a massive amount of material from space around it and so exploded with more force than many supernovae. SN185 is 8,200-9,100 light years away, so it actually exploded nearly 10,000-11,000 years ago.

MOST RECENT – BUT UNNOTICED

Cassiopeia A went supernova around 300 years ago, in about 1688, but there are no reports of it — no one seems to have noticed. It's possible that the white dwarf lost a lot of matter before going supernova, and that material then cloaked the explosion. It's the brightest source of radio waves in the Milky Way and was one of the first noticed, being spotted in 1947.

The bubble of gas and dust from the supernova is expanding at 2,000 km (1,243 miles) per second.

SUPERNOVAE ELSEWHERE

In the Milky Way, there's a supernova event about every 100 years, but not all are visible from Earth. Supernovae don't only happen in our own galaxy, though, and astronomers find many in other galaxies each year. In 1987, astronomers noticed a supernova starting in the Large Magellanic Cloud, a nearby dwarf galaxy. This supernova was 168,000 light years away and just bright enough to be seen with the naked eye.

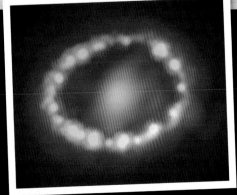

SN1604 is 13,000–20,000 light years away, so the explosion actually happened about 11,000–18,000 years BC, when woolly mammoths still roamed the Earth.

FIRST SPACE TOURIST

DENNIS TITO

Lots of people dream of going into space. We can't all train as astronauts, but those with enough money might be able to go as tourists! The first-ever space tourist was Dennis Tito, who went in the Russian spacecraft Soyuz TM-32 in 2001.

An American engineer and multibillionaire, Tito paid the Russian Space Agency $20 million to fly him to the International Space Station, accompanied by two Russian cosmonauts. NASA objected to the flight, saying having an untrained astronaut on board could be a safety risk.

GOT WHAT IT TAKES?

Tito had previously worked as a NASA engineer, planning missions to Mars and Venus, so he was not a complete space novice. Aged sixty-one at the time of his flight, Tito had watched Sputnik's launch in 1957 when he was a teenager and dreamed of going to space. To train for the launch, he spent time being spun in a centrifuge at eight times the force of gravity.

After months of training in Russia, Tito spent six days on board the International Space Station.

Tito had his spacesuit custom made. He donated it to the Smithsonian Museum in Washington, DC where it is displayed.

FIRST TOURIST TRIP TO SPACE

TOURIST	DENNIS TITO, USA
SPACECRAFT	SOYUZ TM-32
LAUNCH DATE	28 APRIL 2001
DURATION OF MISSION	7 DAYS, 22 HRS, 4 MINS

MORE PLANS

With a fortune of $71 billion, Tito is planning his own manned mission to Mars, but it is unlikely to happen before 2021. Tito hopes to launch a ship carrying two astronauts on a 16-month round trip. The spacecraft will fly to within 100 km (62 miles) of Mars before returning to Earth, but won't land on Mars.

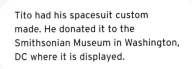

SPACE PLANES

Virgin Galactic is like Virgin Atlantic — but higher! The new Virgin Galactic spacecraft will take tourists into space, above Earth's atmosphere. The ship will launch from a spaceport in New Mexico, USA. The rocket is carried into the air by a plane with two fuselages, then the rocket engine fires after the craft is released, taking it out of Earth's atmosphere.

FIRST ASTEROID KNOWN TO HAVE A MOON

IDA AND DACTYL

The asteroid Ida is the first asteroid known to have its own moon.

The moon, named Dactyl, is a twentieth of the size of Ida and so small you could walk all around it in less than an hour! The probe Galileo visited Ida in 1993. Dactyl was discovered in 1994 when scientists examined the photos sent back from Galileo. Dactyl is egg-shaped, while Ida looks more like a potato.

IDA AND DACTYL

ASTEROID DESIGNATION	243 IDA
SIZE (IDA)	53.6 X 24.0 X 15.2 KM (33.3 X 14.9 X 9.44 MILES)
SIZE (DACTYL)	1.6 X 1.4 X 1.2 KM (0.99 X 0.86 X 0.75 MILES)
LENGTH OF DAY	4 HRS, 38 MINS
ORBITAL PERIOD (YEAR)	1,768 DAYS (4 YRS, 307 DAYS)
DACTYL'S ORBIT	APPROX. 20 HOURS
SURFACE TEMPERATURE	-70 °C (-94 °F)

MAIN-BELT ASTEROIDS

Ida is a main-belt asteroid, which means it orbits the Sun as part of a large band of asteroids between Mars and Jupiter. The asteroid belt is home to innumerable asteroids of all shapes and sizes. The largest, Ceres, is 950 km (590 miles) across and qualifies as a dwarf planet, while the smallest are specks of dust. It is thought that the asteroid belt is made up of material that should have formed a planet, but failed.

 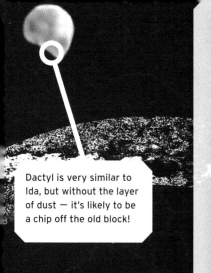

GIANT MOON

Not all moons are tiny like Dactyl. Ganymede, the largest moon in the solar system, is one of Jupiter's moons. It's larger than the planet Mercury, and three quarters the size of Mars, and if it were orbiting the Sun instead of Jupiter scientists would count it as a planet. Ganymede has a core of metal with a layer of rock around it, and then, surrounding the whole, an ice shell 800-km thick over an ocean of liquid water.

Dactyl is very similar to Ida, but without the layer of dust — it's likely to be a chip off the old block!

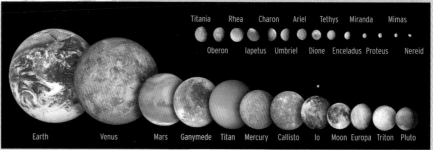

Titania Rhea Charon Ariel Tethys Miranda Mimas

Oberon Iapetus Umbriel Dione Enceladus Proteus Nereid

Earth Venus Mars Ganymede Titan Mercury Callisto Io Moon Europa Triton Pluto

Ida's surface is covered in a layer of smashed rock 50-100 m (164-328 ft) thick.

MANY MORE MOONS

The smallest planetary moon has the unmemorable name of S/2010 J1 and is 1.8 km (1.1 miles) across, barely bigger than Dactyl. But there's no official definition of a moon by size — a moon is anything that orbits something else in the solar system. Technically, every speck of dust in the rings of Saturn and Jupiter is a moon, but it would be tricky to count and name them all — there are millions!

Ida and Dactyl are both so cratered that when anything else hits the surface, the new crater covers up old ones.

PLANET WITH MOST RINGS

SATURN

Saturn is famous for its rings — they extend far out into space but are extremely thin, like a vast circular disc around the planet.

There are five main rings, named G, F, A, B and C (outer to inner), with gaps between them. Each ring is made up of millions or even billions of particles orbiting in clumps that form minor ringlets. The other gas giants also have rings, but they are much fainter and smaller.

🪐 ROAMING RUBBISH

We don't know exactly how the rings formed. They might be left over from when Saturn first formed, 4 billion years ago, or could be only a few hundred million years old. The bits that were too close to the planet to form a big moon are doomed to circle the planet forever. Or they could be the debris from smashed-up moons that collided, or the remnants of a moon torn apart by straying too close to Saturn.

Each ring is only about 1-km (0.62-miles) thick (top to bottom), but the widest ring is 300,000 km (186,410 miles) wide.

Each particle in the rings orbits Saturn like a tiny moon.

RUNNING RINGS

If we could take a close-up look at the rings, we'd see billions of particles, ranging in size from specks of icy dust to lumps the size of mountains, but most are between 1 cm and 10 m (0.4 in and 32.8 ft) across. There are clear gaps between the rings that keep them distinct. Small 'shepherd moons' keep some of the gaps clear, sweeping any stray particles into their own gravitational field.

The rings are not really bright colours — they are made of chunks of water ice. The colours in photos come from the way the images are taken.

PLANET WITH EARS

The astronomer Galileo discovered Saturn's rings in 1610, but he didn't realize they were rings. Instead, he described Saturn as three planets in a row that don't move relative to each other, and with the largest one in the middle. He sketched the system, making Saturn look as though it had ears (right).

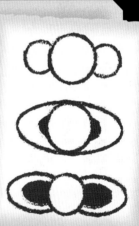

SATURN'S RING SYSTEM

NUMBER OF RINGS	5 MAJOR
RINGS DISCOVERED	1610
MASS OF RINGS	3 X 10^{19} KG (6.6 X 10^{19} LB) — 9 X 10^{19} KG (19.8 X 10^{19} LB)
EXTENT FROM SATURN	18,000,000 KM (11,184,681 MILES)

BIGGEST RING

Saturn's largest and outermost ring is vast. It's very faint, with a low density of matter, but is 12 million km (7.5 million miles) wide. It's unlike the other rings because it is tall as well as wide — it's 20 times the height of Saturn itself. A billion Earths could fit in the ring. The density is so low that there are only about 20 grains of dust per cubic kilometre (per 0.62 cubic miles).

LARGEST WHIRLWIND

JUPITER'S RED SPOT

The biggest whirlwind in the solar system rages in Jupiter's atmosphere of hydrogen and helium.

It has been going for more than 180 years without a pause and possibly more than 350 years. It was first noticed by Cassini in 1665, who described a 'permanent spot' on the planet. The system is not properly a storm, but a vortex – a circular wind system like a hurricane or whirlwind. It covers an area at least twice as wide as the whole Earth – two or three planets Earth's size could be swallowed by it.

Appearing as a giant red spot on Jupiter's surface, the vortex ranges between 25,000–40,000 km (15,534–24,854 miles) across.

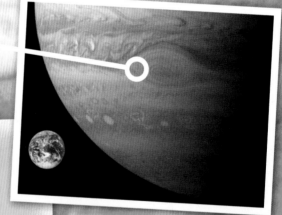

SPOTLIGHT ON THE SPOTS

The Great Red Spot isn't the only spot on Jupiter. Smaller spots are dotted around the bands of Jupiter's atmosphere. One, known as the Baby Red Spot, was engulfed by the Great Red Spot in 2008 when the two collided. Another large vortex, called Oval BA, began as a white spot and turned red in 2006, possibly because of changes in atmospheric pressure. It formed from other colliding spots and is growing, with winds of nearly 620 km/h (385 mph).

STORMS TOO

Although the spot isn't really a storm, Jupiter does have fierce storms. Typically, they last from a few days to a few months. They have lightning and rain, just like storms on Earth, but are much bigger – vertical storms can tower up to 100 km (62 miles), and lightning strikes are several times more powerful than on Earth.

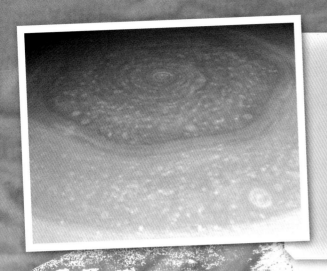

STORMY SATURN

Saturn is another gas giant, not as large as Jupiter but with a vortex almost as big — and stranger still. Near Saturn's north pole is a hexagonal spot 32,000 km (19,884 miles) across, made up of a jet stream surrounding a massive storm blowing at 320 km/h (199 mph). The storm is decades old and may have been raging for hundreds of years. The hurricane at the centre is fifty times the size of large hurricanes on Earth.

The spot spins at about one revolution every six days.

The spot has been monitored continuously since 1831, so we know the winds have been blowing for all that time.

JUPITER'S RED SPOT

DISCOVERED	1665 OR 1831
DIAMETER	UP TO 40,000 KM (24,855 MILES)
WIND SPEED	618 KM/H (384 MPH)
INVESTIGATED BY	GALILEO PROBE

FIRST DWARF PLANET

ERIS

When Eris was discovered in 2003, the International Astronomical Union (IAU) created a new class of planet: dwarf planets.

At first, Eris was thought to be slightly larger than Pluto, and was announced as the tenth planet. Then the IAU realized there might be more and more planets popping up. So they defined a planet for the first time. A planet must be in orbit around the Sun, have enough mass to have become roughly spherical and to have cleared the area around it in its orbit. Under these new rules, Pluto was no longer a planet.

SOLID, LIQUID, GAS

We think of atmosphere as a layer of gas around a planet — that's how our planet works. But the chemicals we know as gases, such as oxygen and nitrogen, chill to a liquid when it is very cold. When it's even colder, they freeze to a solid. When Eris is furthest from the Sun, the atmosphere turns into a film of nitrogen ice.

ERIS	
DISCOVERED	2005
SIZE	2,326 KM
	(1,445 MILES)
	($\frac{1}{4}$ x EARTH)
CURRENT DISTANCE FROM SUN	96.4 AU
CLOSEST TO SUN (IN ABOUT 280 YEARS)	37 AU
ORBITAL PERIOD (YEAR)	557 YEARS
LENGTH OF DAY	26 HOURS

Eris has an eccentric orbit that takes it three times as far from the Sun in its winter than in its summer.

DWARF FAMILY

There are now five accepted dwarf planets: Pluto, Eris, Ceres, Haumea and Makemake. Haumea is the strangest, as it's shaped like a rugby ball, or an American football, and rotates once every four hours — so its day is four hours long, but its year is 310 Earth years! That means there are nearly 680,000 Haumean days in its year.

Ceres

Eris

Pluto

Haumea

Makemake

Eris is a cold and hostile place — its atmosphere is often a frozen glaze over the rocky surface.

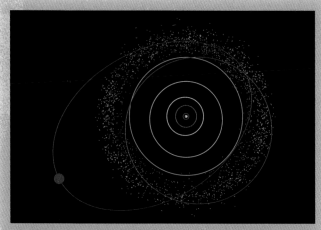

AT HOME IN THE KUIPER BELT AND BEYOND

Pluto, Haumea and Makemake orbit inside the Kuiper Belt. It's a wide ring-shaped region of space beyond Neptune (30-55 AU from the Sun), where frozen chunks of water, methane and ammonia orbit the Sun. There are possibly 100,000 Kuiper Belt Objects more than 100 km (62 miles) across, and a trillion all together. Eris is remote enough to stray outside the Kuiper Belt.

When Eris is furthest from the Sun, it takes up to 12 $^3/_4$ hours for sunlight to reach it.

BIGGEST GALAXY

IC 1101

The largest known galaxy has the uninspiring name of IC 1101. It's a billion light years away from us and is around six million light years across.

By contrast, the Milky Way is only 100,000 light years across, so IC 1101 is 50-60 times as wide as the Milky Way. If the Milky Way were the size of your thumbnail, IC 1101 would be longer than your whole arm. IC 1101 has the mass of 100 trillion stars – that's about 2,000 times the mass of the Milky Way.

BIG, BIGGER AND BIGGEST

Galaxies come in different shapes and sizes, but they are all huge. The smallest are dwarf galaxies. Small in astronomical terms, they usually have several billions stars. The smallest of them are ultra-compact dwarfs, which only have about 100 million stars and are only 200 light years across. Spiral galaxies are medium-sized. The Milky Way is an example of a spiral galaxy with 300 billion stars. Even larger galaxies are elliptical, and the very largest are nearly spherical — including IC 1101 (below).

IC 1101 is a giant elliptical galaxy in the constellation Serpens.

The yellow-red tint of IC 1101 tells astronomers that most of its stars are quite old, and relatively few new stars are forming.

MAKING GALAXIES

Dwarf galaxies are often new galaxies, with relatively few stars. The stars shine with a blue light early in their life. Many dwarf galaxies orbit larger galaxies, but some are torn apart by the force of their larger neighbours, destroyed in collisions, or absorbed by larger galaxies. The galaxies that absorb the dwarfs slowly get larger.

WHAT'S THE DIFFERENCE?

IC 1101 has about a trillion stars — but the mass of 100 trillion stars. How does that work? We only know the nature of a tiny proportion of the universe. A lot of its mass is taken up by mysterious dark matter and dark energy. Part of IC 1101's mass is in the form of a super-massive black hole at its centre — one of the most massive black holes in the universe.

IC 1101 contains around a trillion stars, which is between three and ten times as many stars as are in the Milky Way.

IC 1101

DISTANCE FROM EARTH	1 BILLION LIGHT YEARS
DISCOVERED	1790

BIGGEST VOLCANO IN THE SOLAR SYSTEM

OLYMPUS MONS

Olympus Mons towers over the landscape of Mars, and was built up from the lava that poured out of it over millions of years. As a shield volcano, it leaked red-hot molten rock when it erupted — rather than hurling its lava upwards.

Olympus Mons covers an area similar in size to France, and is three times as tall as Mount Everest, the tallest mountain on Earth. It is 100 times the volume of the largest shield volcano on Earth, Mauna Loa in Hawaii.

The sides have a long, shallow slope. Walking up Olympus Mons would feel like a stroll up a gentle hill.

LONG HISTORY

Olympus Mons has formed over the last three billion years through a series of eruptions. There are six craters visible in the caldera, suggesting there have been at least six eruptions during that time. The volcano might still be active and could erupt again.

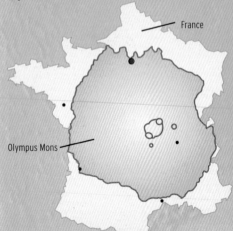

France

Olympus Mons

OLYMPUS MONS

DIAMETER	600 KM (373 MILES)
HEIGHT	22 KM (14 MILES)
AGE	3.7 BILLION YEARS
LAST ERUPTION	25-45 MILLION YEARS AGO

SHIELD VOLCANOES

Olympus Mons is a shield volcano, like the island volcanoes on Hawaii. Shield volcanoes are fed by a 'hotspot' — a gap in the Earth's crust through which molten rock can leak from underneath. On Earth, the crust is slowly moving all the time, and so shield volcanoes form in chains — eventually, the bit of land that was over the hotspot moves away and another area moves over the hotspot, starting a new shield volcano. On Mars, the crust does not move, so the same area stays over the hotspot forever.

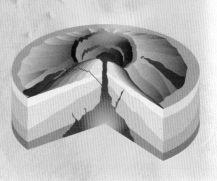

The surface is covered with traces of previous lava flows that look like rivers, but it hasn't erupted for 25 million years.

TALLEST MOUNTAIN

Rheasilvia is the tallest mountain in the solar system, and sits on Vesta, an asteroid 525 km (326 miles) across. Although Vesta is the second most massive asteroid in the solar system, it is small to host such a large mountain. Rheasilvia stands inside an impact crater 505 km (314 miles) across, near Vesta's south pole. The walls of the crater are 31 km (19 miles) tall, and the mountain rises 25 km (15.5 miles) in its centre.

The top has a caldera, or crater, 80 km (50 miles) wide. This is where the lava has risen to the surfaced and poured out of the volcano when it has been active.

MOST DISTANT
SOLAR SYSTEM BODY

SEDNA

Sedna is a rocky planetoid, possibly a dwarf planet. It strays further from the Sun than any other known planetoid or asteroid, going so far away that it takes nearly five and a half days for sunlight to reach it.

Its orbit is a wide ellipse with the Sun and planets clustered at one end. In 2075 or 2076, Sedna will be at its closest to the Sun (perihelion) for 11,400 years. At the other end of its orbit (aphelion) it is 13 times as far away at 937 AU (one AU, or Astronomical Unit, is the distance from the Earth to the Sun).

NOT ALONE

Sedna is not the only far-distant planetoid. In 2012 VP113, first observed in 2012, overlaps Sedna's orbit. Although it never comes as close to the Sun as Sedna, being 80 AU away at perihelion, it does not stray as far out as Sedna with 450 AU its most distant. Its orbit takes around 4,300 years. Some scientists believe there might be many more distant planetoids still undiscovered — perhaps as many as 1,000.

The surface is rocky, with a red tinge, and very cold: -261 °C (-437.8 F).

MONSTER PLANET?

The strange orbits of Sedna and 2012 VP113 have led some astronomers to suggest there might be an undiscovered giant planet lying far beyond the known planets. It would receive so little light from the Sun that it is not visible. More likely causes of the odd orbits are a passing star or rogue planet from outside the solar system tugging the planetoids away from the Sun.

Sedna is about a tenth the diameter of Earth: if Earth were the size of an apple, Sedna would be the size of a grape.

Sedna is so far from the Sun that if you visited it, the Sun would be hard to distinguish from other stars in the sky.

SEDNA

DIAMETER	995 KM (618 MILES)
ORBIT (LENGTH OF YEAR)	11,400 YEARS
CLOSEST APPROACH TO SUN	76 AU
FURTHEST DISTANCE TO SUN	937 AU

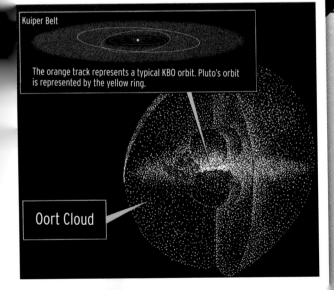

Kuiper Belt

The orange track represents a typical KBO orbit. Pluto's orbit is represented by the yellow ring.

Oort Cloud

TOWARDS THE OORT CLOUD

Sedna is in an empty area called the Scattered Disc outside the Kuiper Belt. Beyond the Scattered Disc, the Oort Cloud is a spherical shell of a cloud that holds many ice asteroids on very long orbits around the sun. Some long-period comets probably come from the Oort Cloud, returning over hundreds of thousands, or even millions, of years.

ODDEST MOON

ATLAS

One of the strangest moons in the solar system is Atlas, a moon of Saturn. While most moons are at least roughly spherical, Atlas looks as though it has a thick, solid ring of rock stuck around its middle.

It's thought that Atlas has grown into its flying-saucer shape because dust from the faint ring that shares its orbit collects around the middle of the moon, building up into a thick belt of rock.

Atlas has never been visited by a probe; the nearest flyby was Cassini in 2005 at nearly 6,200 km (3,852.5 miles).

 PILOT MOONS

Saturn's rings are kept in order by pilot or shepherd moons. These have orbits on the edge of a ring, and their gravity sweeps up any stray dust, rock or ice, dragging it in with their gravity. Rings that are near others have a crisp edge, rather than blurring together, because these moons keep clear gaps between them. But some moons have much larger gaps with no moons — no one knows why these ones are clear.

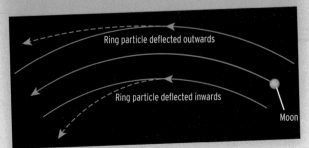

Ring particle deflected outwards

Ring particle deflected inwards

Moon

ATLAS	
DISCOVERED	1980
ORBITAL PERIOD	14 HRS, 24 MINS
DIAMETER	32 KM (20 MILES)

Most moons are detected from photos taken by probes or telescopes, such as the Hubble Space Telescope (see pp. 16-17). Many have been found from photos taken by the Cassini spacecraft. There are thousands of images to hunt through, and each moon is not always visible — sometimes it is hidden behind its planet. Scientists compare photos of a planet taken at different times to spot tiny moons and work out how long they take to orbit the planet.

Atlas is one of the moons closest to Saturn and its orbit takes less than a day, even though Saturn is a large planet.

Although Atlas is on the edge of Saturn's A ring, it's not — as first thought — a shepherd moon for it.

PLASTIC MOON?

Another of Saturn's moons, Titan, has naturally-occurring plastic on its surface! In 2014, scientists found evidence of propylene, which is used on Earth to make plastic food containers, car bumpers and other items. It is made by the action of sunlight on the methane in Titan's atmosphere.

MOST FAMOUS
ANIMAL TO GO INTO SPACE

LAIKA ON SPUTNIK 2

Although lots of animals have gone into space, the most famous is certainly Laika the dog, who became the first animal to orbit the Earth in 1957.

She wore a special harness, and was strapped into the spacecraft so that she could not move around during the flight and hurt herself. There was no way of getting a spacecraft safely back to Earth at the time, the capsule broke up on re-entry into Earth's atmosphere on 4 April 1958.

 ### A DOG'S BIOG

Laika was a stray that was found on the streets of Moscow. She was a mongrel, possibly part terrier and part husky, about three years old at the time of her flight. She trained with two other dogs, one of whom became the back-up choice. 'Training' consisted of keeping them in increasingly small cages for up to 20 days to get used to being confined in a cramped space. The cruelty of sending Laika into space has been criticized since, and animals in space are better treated now.

The capsule was very small and Laika didn't have space to move around at all — she had been prepared for inactivity during training.

 ### LIFE AND DEATH

Although it was clear from the start that Laika would die in space, she was expected to live longer than she did. For years, the USSR reported that she died of lack of oxygen, or that she was killed with a poisoned meal when the oxygen was about to run out. In fact, she died after just a few hours when the capsule overheated.

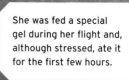

She was fed a special gel during her flight and, although stressed, ate it for the first few hours.

LAIKA ON SPUTNIK 2

LAUNCH	3 NOVEMBER, 1957
DEATH	3 NOVEMBER, 1957
LAUNCHED FROM	USSR
AGE	3 YEARS
WEIGHT	5 KG (11 LB)

Laika had sensors attached to monitor her heart rate and breathing during the flight.

🪐 TOP DOG

Laika's mission paved the way for human space flight. The readings from the sensors attached to Laika showed that although her heart rate increased to three times its normal rate at launch, it returned to normal, and she survived both the launch and being weightless. Belka and Strelka were the next dogs in space, in 1960, and they survived the trip.

FASTEST SPACECRAFT

JUNO

The fastest speed reached by any spacecraft is 40 km per second (25 miles per second) or 144,000 km/h (89,477.5 mph) — the speed achieved by the NASA spacecraft Juno on its way to Jupiter.

Juno managed this speed by using a 'gravity assist' manoeuvre using the Earth as a slingshot to hurl it far into space. Juno was in space for two years before the gravity assist manoeuvre sent it whirling towards Jupiter.

 ## THE JUNO MISSION

Juno's path took it in a huge figure-9 shape, with a complete, wide orbit of the Sun before it headed off towards Jupiter and arrived in 2016. It will orbit Jupiter, taking photographs and readings, before eventually descending into the gas giant. It will investigate Jupiter's thick atmosphere, measuring how much water is present and providing information about how Jupiter formed. It will also explore the planet's magnetic and gravitational fields.

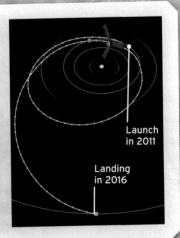

Launch in 2011

Landing in 2016

JUNO	
LAUNCH	5 AUGUST 2011
ARRIVAL AT JUPITER	5 JULY 2016
SIZE	20 M X 4.5 M (66 FT X 15 FT)
TARGET FOR LAST RESEARCH	5,000 KM (3107 MILES) ABOVE JUPITER
END OF MISSION	BURN UP ON DESCENT INTO JUPITER
DURATION OF MISSION	6 YEARS

Juno spins constantly at three revolutions per minute as it travels through space. Spinning makes it more stable.

Spacecraft outbound velocity

Jupiter

Spacecraft inbound velocity

CATAPULTED BY GRAVITY

A gravity assist or gravity slingshot manoeuvre uses the gravitational pull of a planet to speed up a passing spacecraft. It works like this: the planet's gravity pulls the spacecraft towards it, making it go faster and faster, but its path is calculated so that instead of crashing into the planet, the spacecraft whizzes past. It uses the acceleration it has gained from the planet's gravity to send it catapulting into space.

By the time Juno gets to Jupiter, the solar panels will be generating less than 500 watts of power – less than the power used by a toaster.

Juno has three huge solar panels, each nearly 9 m (30 ft) long, to collect energy from sunlight to power it.

LEGO ON JUPITER!

As well as its scientific instruments, Juno carries a metal plaque bearing a picture of the astronomer Galileo and some text in his handwriting describing his discovery of the moons of Jupiter in 1610. It also carries three LEGO figures: one of Galileo and one of the Roman god Jupiter and his wife Juno. Although most LEGO is plastic these were specially made of aluminium. NASA and LEGO thought these figures might encourage more children to be interested in science, technology and space.

MOST DISTANT OBJECT

Z8_GND_5296

The most distant known object is a galaxy 30 billion light years away. It has the dull name z8_GND_5296.

We see the galaxy as it looked 700 million years after the start of the universe, when it was very new. From studying the light, scientists can tell that it was quite a small galaxy, about 1-2% the size of the Milky Way and was making stars at a very rapid rate. It is a glimpse into the early life of a galaxy.

TIME AND SPACE

Light travels at 299,792 km per second (186,282 miles per second) – just over a billion km per hour (just over 600 million miles per hour) – and the light from z8_GND_5296 has taken more than 13 billion years to reach Earth! In fact, we don't know whether the galaxy is still around – it could have been destroyed billions of years ago, but we wouldn't know yet.

We see z8_GND_5296 in the position it occupied 13.1 billion years ago – it's been moving ever since, so it's not there now.

z8_GND_5296 was making new stars at a rate of around 300 a year.

Z8_GND_5296

DISCOVERED	OCTOBER 2013
AGE	13.1 BILLION YEARS
DISTANCE FROM EARTH	30 BILLION LIGHT YEARS
MASS	1 BILLION X SUN

EXPANDING UNIVERSE

z8_GND_5296 is now even further away – 30 billion light years distant. Because the universe is expanding rapidly, the galaxy has been pushed much further away by intervening space since the light from it started its journey. The furthest we can possibly see is about 45 billion light years away – the edge of what's called the 'observable universe' or the 'visible universe'. But that doesn't mean there is nothing further away, just that we can't see it.

It was discovered using visible light and infrared images taken by the Hubble Space Telescope.

BEGINNING AND END

Soon after the Big Bang, z8_GND_5296 began creating stars. We know about the start of the universe, but what about the end? The current period of forming stars might last up to a hundred billion years. Then the whole sequence of stars being created and dying will slowly stop over, perhaps, ten to a hundred trillion years. After that, the cold, dark remnants of stars might fall into super-massive black holes or be blasted off into space as they collide with each other.

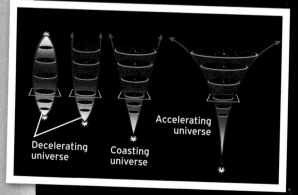

Decelerating universe

Coasting universe

Accelerating universe

THE BIGGEST
TREASURE HUNT EVER

KEPLER'S EXOPLANET HUNT

The search for life on planets orbiting other stars is carried out using the space telescope Kepler, which is constantly monitoring one area of the sky.

Exoplanets are planets that orbit other stars, outside our solar system. Astronomers are especially interested in exoplanets that are similar to Earth. Some are gas giants, like Jupiter and Saturn. Others are Earth-like planets with a hard, rocky surface. If they had an atmosphere and liquid water, some of them might host life of a type we would recognize.

The Kepler telescope watches an area of sky near the constellation Cygnus, which contains 145,000 stars — just a tiny fragment of our galaxy.

HUNTING FOR PLANETS

Astronomers hunt for exoplanets by watching the stars in Kepler's field of view and spotting a periodic dip in the amount of light coming from a star. This can be caused by a planet passing in front of its star as it orbits. From the change in light, scientists can work outwhat the planet is made of. The gap reveals its orbit and how far it is from its star.

Astronomers have identified thousands of possible exoplanets in the area, mostly one per star — but some stars appear to have more than one planet.

Not all planets are in an orbit that can be seen by Kepler. Small planets have a 1-in-200 chance of being visible, and big planets a 1-in-10 chance.

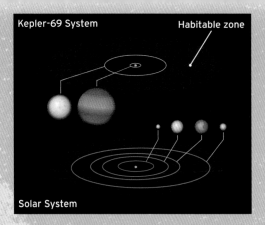

Kepler-69 System

Habitable zone

Solar System

LIVING IN THE GOLDILOCKS ZONE

Remember the story of the three bears? Goldilocks found Daddy Bear's porridge too hot, and Mummy Bear's porridge too cold, but Baby Bear's porridge was just right. The area around a star where an Earth-like planet would be the right temperature to support life is called the Goldilocks zone because it's neither too hot nor too cold for liquid water to exist on the surface. It's also called the habitable zone.

Scientists are still finding exoplanets. In August 2018, NASA announced a total of 2,327 planets!

KEPLER'S EXOPLANET HUNT

LAUNCH	7 MARCH 2009
MISSION DURATION	3.5 YEARS (CAN BE EXTENDED TO 7.5 YEARS)
TELESCOPE SIZE	0.95-M (3.11-FT)-DIAMETER PHOTOMETER
MASS	1,071 KG (2,361 LB)

CRUNCHING THE NUMBERS

More exoplanet candidates are discovered all the time. So far there around 100 confirmed planets in habitable zones, of which around a quarter are less than twice Earth's size. Calculations suggest around 20% of sun-like stars have an Earth-like planet, so there could be 100 billion Earth-like planets in the Milky Way.

MOST DEVASTATING
ASTEROID STRIKE [WE THINK]

CHICXULUB STRIKE

When a fast-moving body crashes into the Earth it can have devastating effects. The most catastrophic space-body strike (we think) happened 65.5 million years ago. It contributed to a mass extinction, killing off most dinosaurs and many other animals and plants.

Many scientists think that dinosaurs became extinct when a large asteroid or comet crashed into what we now think of as Mexico. The impact would have started forest fires and produced gas, ash and dust that could have blocked out the Sun, causing a cold period. It's likely that other causes, including climate change and volcanic eruptions, also contributed to the mass extinction.

The impact might have been caused by either a massive asteroid or a comet.

WHAT DIED?

All non-avian dinoasurs (that is, all non-flying dinosaurs) died out. So did the water-dwelling reptiles, called plesiosaurs and ichthyosaurs, and the flying reptiles called pterosaurs. Ammonites, many plants and even tiny plankton in the sea were killed off. In all, 70-80% of all species died.

CHICXULUB STRIKE

DATE OF IMPACT	65.5 MILLION YEARS AGO
SIZE	APPROX. 10 KM (6.2 MILES) ACROSS
POSSIBLE SUSPECTS	ASTEROID OR COMET

FLYING ROCKS

Asteroids are minor planets, or planetoids. They orbit the Sun, and vary in size from nearly 1,000 km (621 miles) across at the largest to just tens of metres. Meteoroids are much smaller, and are up to one metre (0.62 miles) across – some are just grains of rock. If a rock from space lands on Earth, it is called a meteorite. Any bits that burn up in the atmosphere as shooting stars are meteors. Comets are made of rock dust and ice.

If it was an asteroid, parts would have burned up as it entered Earth's atmosphere. Chunks of burning rock would start forest fires.

If it was a comet, it would have been like a giant, dirty snowball made of ice, dust and fragments of rock. No large chunks would have been left over.

IMPACT

Whatever struck Earth in the Yucatán peninsula in Mexico, it created a crater 180-km (112-miles) wide called Chicxulub. A layer of the metal iridium is found all over the Earth, which was laid down 65 million years ago, at the time of the impact. Iridium is rare on Earth but common in asteroids. If an asteroid vaporized on impact, the iridium could be widely scattered. But iridium is also ejected in volcanic eruptions – so we can't be sure where it came from.

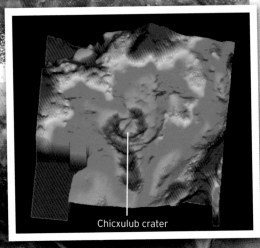
Chicxulub crater

FIRST FLYBY
OF ANOTHER PLANET

MARINER 2

The very first flyby of another planet was the Mariner 2 Venus mission in 1962. The spacecraft, launched from the USA, took four months to reach Venus.

The object of the mission was to collect data about the atmosphere and climate on Venus, and to make measurements on the journey. Mariner provided an accurate measurement of the AU, which is the distance from Earth to the Sun. It also discovered that in interplanetary space, the solar wind streams continuously, and there is less dust than there is near to Earth.

MARINER 1

Mariner 2 was a back-up craft. The mission to Venus was planned for Mariner 1, but the two-stage rocket used for its launch veered off course on 22 July 1962 and it was destroyed with a remotely controlled explosion. The launch error was caused by a bug in the program controlling Mariner 1 from the ground and a defective signal from the launch rocket.

Two solar panels, each under 2 m (6.6 ft) long and 76 cm (30 in) wide, collected solar power for the spacecraft.

MARINER 2

LAUNCH DATE	27 AUGUST 1962
MASS	202.8 KG (447 LB)
SIZE	5.05-M (16.5 FT) SPAN (SOLAR PANELS) X 3.66 M (12 FT)
MISSION DURATION	129 DAYS

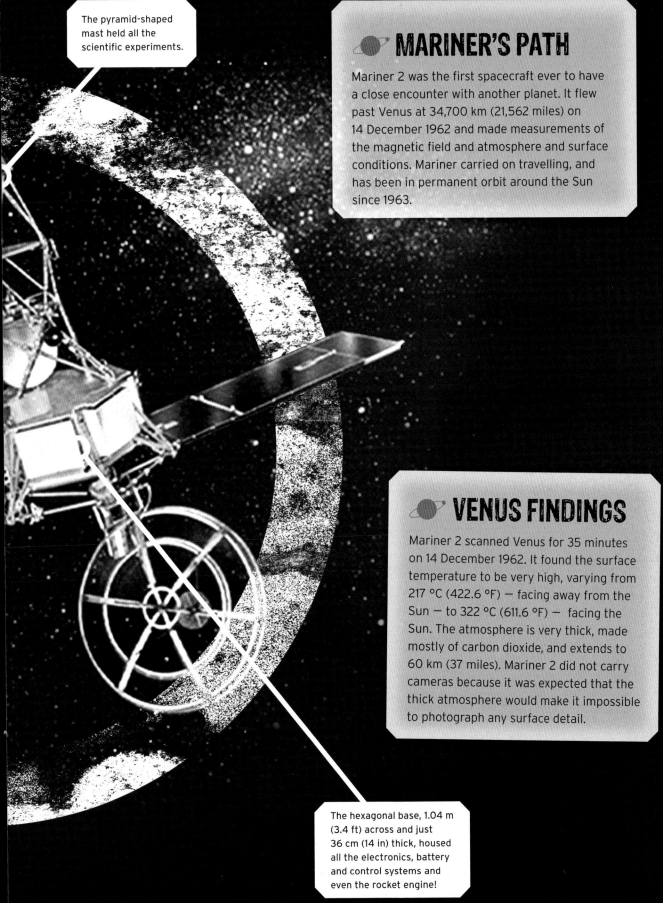

The pyramid-shaped mast held all the scientific experiments.

MARINER'S PATH

Mariner 2 was the first spacecraft ever to have a close encounter with another planet. It flew past Venus at 34,700 km (21,562 miles) on 14 December 1962 and made measurements of the magnetic field and atmosphere and surface conditions. Mariner carried on travelling, and has been in permanent orbit around the Sun since 1963.

VENUS FINDINGS

Mariner 2 scanned Venus for 35 minutes on 14 December 1962. It found the surface temperature to be very high, varying from 217 °C (422.6 °F) — facing away from the Sun — to 322 °C (611.6 °F) — facing the Sun. The atmosphere is very thick, made mostly of carbon dioxide, and extends to 60 km (37 miles). Mariner 2 did not carry cameras because it was expected that the thick atmosphere would make it impossible to photograph any surface detail.

The hexagonal base, 1.04 m (3.4 ft) across and just 36 cm (14 in) thick, housed all the electronics, battery and control systems and even the rocket engine!

MOST DISTANT PLANET

NEPTUNE

Neptune is further from the Sun than any other planet in our solar system. With so little light and heat reaching it, Neptune is a cold, dark world.

Neptune is so far from the Sun that it takes nearly 165 Earth years to complete a single orbit of the Sun. That means that on Neptune, no one would have a birthday because we'd all live less than a year! At the outer edges of the atmosphere, the temperature is -218 °C (-360.4 °F) – one of the coldest places in the solar system. But at the centre (core) the pressure is so great the temperature is 5,000 °C (9,032 °F), which is similar to the surface of the Sun.

GIANT SNOWBALL

Like Uranus, Neptune is an 'ice giant'. Its atmosphere has hydrogen and helium at the top, with methane, water and ammonia further down, forced under pressure to become a thick, sludge – it's like ice, but hot! Near the centre, the pressure is so great that the chemicals break down and the carbon from them might form a lake of liquid diamond.

Traces of the gas methane in the outer atmosphere give Neptune a blue tinge.

STORMY WEATHER

Neptune's Great Dark Spot seen by Voyager 2 in 1989 was a vast system of winds whirling at up to 2,100 km/h (1,305 mph) – the fastest winds anywhere in the solar system. The system moves westwards across Neptune at 1,200 km/h (746 mph). Today, though, that spot seems to have disappeared and new spots have come and gone. Unlike Jupiter's storms, which may last up to centuries, Neptune's weather changes much faster.

FOUND BY MATHS

Earth

Neptune

Neptune is the first planet to have been predicted before it was discovered. In the 1820s, astronomers noticed that the orbit of Uranus didn't match their predictions. They worked out that the gravity of an unknown planet must be disrupting its orbit. Neptune wasn't found until 1846 when the Berlin Observatory searched a patch of sky where the French astronomer, Urbain le Verrier, predicted that it should be. Only one Neptunian year has passed since the planet was discovered.

Neptune's faint and fragmented ring system was spotted by Voyager 2 in 1989.

The Great Dark Spot and Small Dark Spot are gigantic storms raging in Neptune's atmosphere.

NEPTUNE

DISCOVERY	1846
DISTANCE FROM SUN	30.1 AU
VISITED	FLYBY, VOYAGER 2, 25 AUGUST 1989
MOONS	14
MASS	1.0243 X 10^{26} KG (2.2581 X 10^{26} LB) (= 17 X EARTH)
DIAMETER	49,528 KM (30,775 MILES) (= 3.9 X EARTH)
LENGTH OF DAY	16 HRS, 6 MINS
LENGTH OF YEAR	164.79 YEARS

BIGGEST KNOWN OBJECT IN THE UNIVERSE

LARGE QUASAR GROUP

Nothing in the universe is as large as the Large Quasar Group (LQG), which is four billion light years across.

For light to get from one side to the other would take almost as long as the Earth has been in existence. LQGs have been found before. This one earns its name from being much, much bigger than the others. It extends to 5% of the entire observable universe.

FEEDING BLACK HOLES

A quasar is a very bright, active area at the heart of a giant galaxy that beams out electromagnetic radiation of all types, including visible light. At the centre of the quasar is a super-massive black hole. Around the black hole, an accretion disk forms – a circular area of matter whizzing around the black hole. As matter is pulled into the black hole, it emits light and other radiation, giving the quasar its brightness.

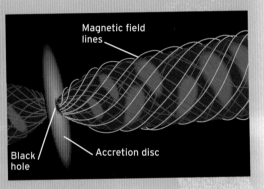
Magnetic field lines
Black hole
Accretion disc

HUGE LARGE QUASAR GROUP

DISCOVERY	2013
DISTANCE FROM EARTH (NEAREST POINT)	9 BILLION LIGHT YEARS
SIZE	4.3 BILLION LIGHT YEARS ACROSS (AT WIDEST POINT)

The huge LQG is more than a million times the mass of the Milky Way and 40,000 times as wide.

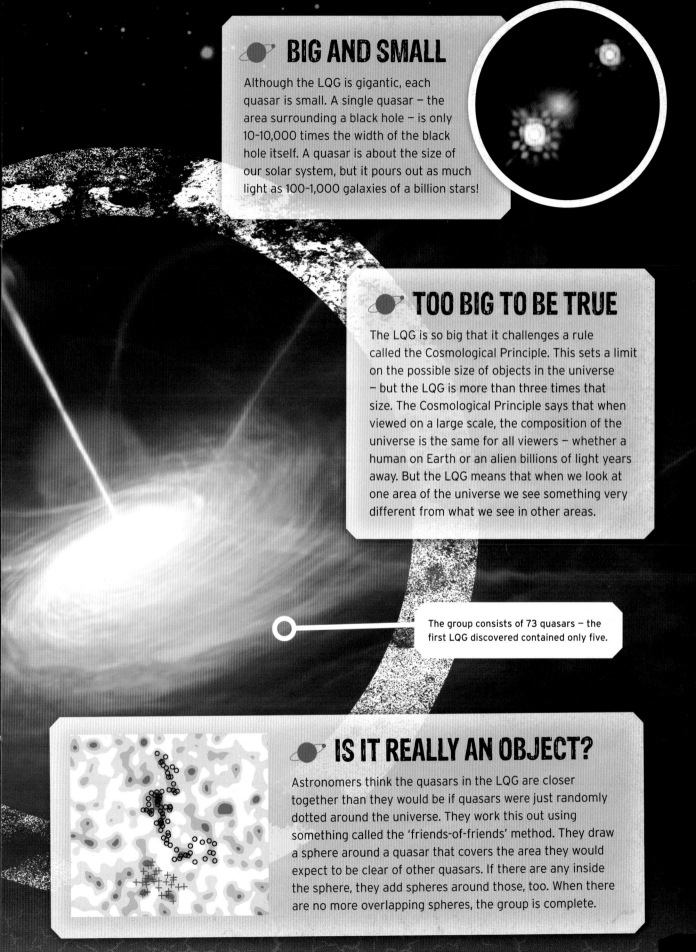

BIG AND SMALL

Although the LQG is gigantic, each quasar is small. A single quasar – the area surrounding a black hole – is only 10-10,000 times the width of the black hole itself. A quasar is about the size of our solar system, but it pours out as much light as 100-1,000 galaxies of a billion stars!

TOO BIG TO BE TRUE

The LQG is so big that it challenges a rule called the Cosmological Principle. This sets a limit on the possible size of objects in the universe – but the LQG is more than three times that size. The Cosmological Principle says that when viewed on a large scale, the composition of the universe is the same for all viewers – whether a human on Earth or an alien billions of light years away. But the LQG means that when we look at one area of the universe we see something very different from what we see in other areas.

The group consists of 73 quasars – the first LQG discovered contained only five.

IS IT REALLY AN OBJECT?

Astronomers think the quasars in the LQG are closer together than they would be if quasars were just randomly dotted around the universe. They work this out using something called the 'friends-of-friends' method. They draw a sphere around a quasar that covers the area they would expect to be clear of other quasars. If there are any inside the sphere, they add spheres around those, too. When there are no more overlapping spheres, the group is complete.

FIRST MISSION
TO LAND ON A COMET

ROSETTA

The first spacecraft to land on a comet was Rosetta, which arrived on Churyumov-Gerasimenko in 2014.

Rosetta was launched in 2004 and spent ten years flying by Earth and Mars before heading out into space to wait for the comet to approach the Sun. It then set a course for the comet, intercepting it in the summer of 2014 and then sending its lander to the surface. Rosetta accompanied the comet until the end of the mission in September 2016, when it was guided onto the comet and communication terminated.

TINY COMET

Churyumov-Gerasimenko is only 4 km (2.5 miles) across. Being so small, it has very little gravity. To prevent Rosetta's lander module, Philae, from drifting off into space, it had 'ice screws' to fix itself to the comet's surface. Philae had instruments on board to drill up to 23 cm (9 in) into the surface in order to take samples from different depths to be analysed. Information about what the comet is made of will be used over many years to help scientists uncover the early history of the solar system.

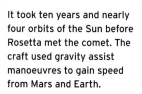

It took ten years and nearly four orbits of the Sun before Rosetta met the comet. The craft used gravity assist manoeuvres to gain speed from Mars and Earth.

ROSETTA

LAUNCHED	2 MARCH 2004
HIBERNATION	957 DAYS
GRAVITY-ASSIST MANOEUVRES	1 X MARS, 3 X EARTH
LANDING ON CHURYUMOV-GERASIMENKO	11 NOVEMBER 2014
PERIOD OF OPERATION ON COMET	2 MONTHS
MISSION DURATION	4595 DAYS (12.5 YEARS)

Two wide wings with solar panels provide Rosetta's only source of power.

The craft carried a separate lander module called Philae to descend to the surface of the comet.

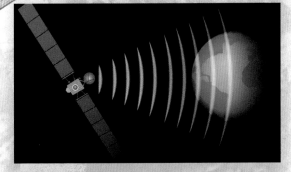

A BIG SLEEP

Rosetta went to sleep – into deep-space hibernation – for a period of 31 months on the way to its rendezvous with Churyumov-Gerasimenko. While 'asleep', Rosetta travelled a distance of 800 million km (497 million miles) from the Sun. When it was too far from the Sun for sunlight to power its solar panels, the craft hibernated. It was woken up on 20 January 2014.

OOPS!

In November 2007, during Rosetta's second flyby of the Earth, it was mistaken for a near-Earth asteroid 20 m (66 ft) across. It was given the name 2007 VN84, and astronomers calculated it would come within 5,700 km (3,542 miles) of Earth. This is an extremely close approach for an asteroid, and sparked concern that it could crash into Earth. An astronomer then realized the path of 2007 VN84 was actually the path of Rosetta!

MOST DISTANT MESSAGE CARRIED FROM EARTH

VOYAGER 2 GOLDEN RECORD

The Golden Record is an audio and photo disc that was sent with both Voyager crafts. Now that Voyager 2 is travelling beyond the solar system, its Golden Record is the most distant message ever sent from Earth.

The Golden Record holds audio recordings of sounds from Earth, and photographs of many Earth scenes, plants, animals and humans. The engraving on the front of the disk shows where Earth is and how to play the disk.

SEE AND HEAR US

The disk contains many diagrams and photos to explain what Earth and its plants and animals are like, how we live, what we know and how to use the disk. It has recordings of natural sounds from whale music to thunderstorms, and spoken messages in 55 old and current languages, including Akkadian, spoken 4,000 years ago in ancient Sumeria.

The starburst picture shows the position of our sun in relation to 14 known neutron stars that emit electromagnetic radiation. The frequency of the pulsars is given to help aliens locate us.

WHO'S LISTENING?

While the Golden Records are messages sent deliberately into space, all our radio and TV broadcasts also leak out into space. They are not strong signals, but by now traces of the earliest broadcasts will have reached more than 100 light years into space in all directions. It would be enough for any intelligent life to realize these were meaningful transmissions.

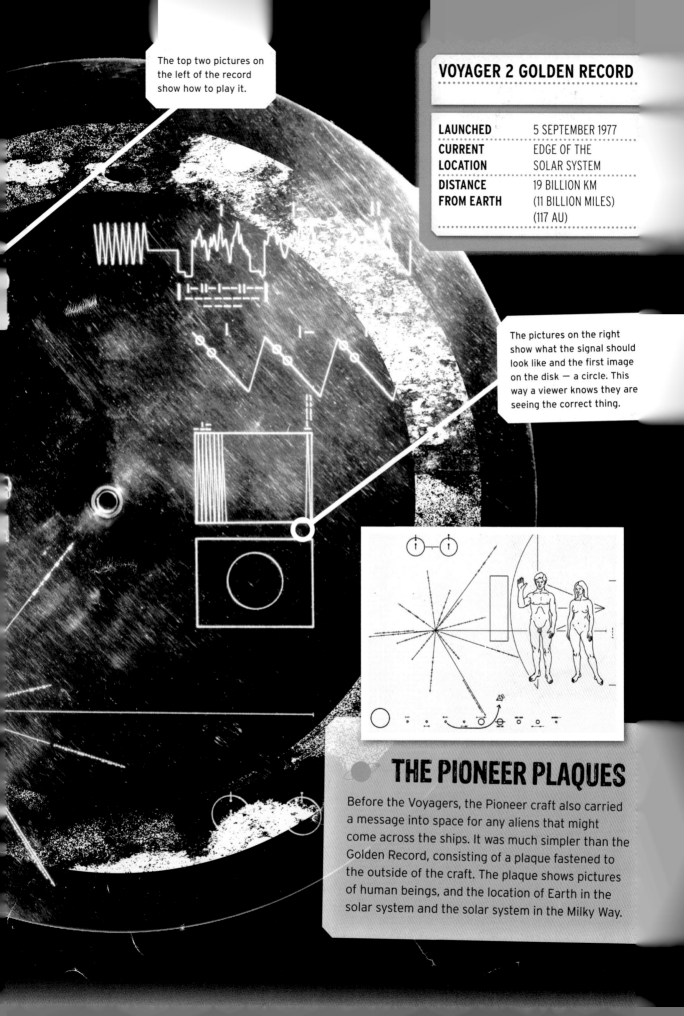

The top two pictures on the left of the record show how to play it.

VOYAGER 2 GOLDEN RECORD

LAUNCHED	5 SEPTEMBER 1977
CURRENT LOCATION	EDGE OF THE SOLAR SYSTEM
DISTANCE FROM EARTH	19 BILLION KM (11 BILLION MILES) (117 AU)

The pictures on the right show what the signal should look like and the first image on the disk — a circle. This way a viewer knows they are seeing the correct thing.

THE PIONEER PLAQUES

Before the Voyagers, the Pioneer craft also carried a message into space for any aliens that might come across the ships. It was much simpler than the Golden Record, consisting of a plaque fastened to the outside of the craft. The plaque shows pictures of human beings, and the location of Earth in the solar system and the solar system in the Milky Way.

FURTHEST TRAVELLING ROVER

OPPORTUNITY

The longest-serving rover is Opportunity, roaming over the surface of Mars since 25 January 2004 — and still there.

Opportunity was carried to Mars by Mars Exploration Rover (MER). It accidentally landed in a crater, which NASA didn't know existed, and ended up 25 m (82 ft) from the planned landing site. Opportunity takes photographs, drills rocks, collects dust and examines the surface to help us learn more about the history and structure of Mars. Since June 2018, dust storms on Mars have put Opportunity into hibernation.

BEYOND THE CALL OF DUTY

Opportunity was scheduled to spend 90 Martian days – called 'sol' – travelling over the surface and collecting data. By 2018, it had over-run its original mission by 13 years and was still sending data back to Earth. Opportunity doesn't race over the surface; its average speed is 30 m (98 ft) a day – but even that makes it the fastest Mars rover there has ever been.

STUCK!

From April to June 2005, Opportunity was stuck in a sand dune, with several of its wheels buried. Mission control on Earth made models and simulations to work out how best to free it – doing the wrong thing could have got the vehicle even more stuck. By moving it just a few centimetres (inches) at a time, it was freed.

Pieces of metal from the fallen World Trade Center in New York are built into Opportunity and its sister rover, Spirit.

 # AMONGST FRIENDS

Opportunity is not alone on Mars. Spirit, on the same ship as Opportunity, stopped working on 26 January 2010. Other dead rovers are Sojourner, stationary since 1997, and two Prop-M Rovers, which landed in 1971 but never worked. Curiosity landed on 6 August 2012 and is still working.

The solar arrays generate about 140 watts for four hours of each Martian day and charge lithium ion batteries to power Opportunity at night.

OPPORTUNITY

LAUNCHED	7 JULY 2003
ACTIVE SINCE	25 JANUARY 2004
AVERAGE SPEED	0.03 KM (0.02 MILES)/DAY
MASS	180 KG (397 LB)
SIZE	1.5-M (4.9-FT) HIGH X 2.3-M (7.5-FT) WIDE X 1.6-M (5.2-FT) LONG
DISTANCE TRAVELLED (ON 14 AUG 2018)	45.16 KM (28 MILES)

Six wheels help Opportunity roll over rocky, uneven ground without falling over.

LARGEST SINGLE-DISH RADIO TELESCOPE

ARECIBO OBSERVATORY

Many astronomical bodies emit radio waves. By measuring the signals with radio dishes, scientists can work out a lot about the distance and composition of the bodies.

The largest single-dish radio telescope on Earth is the Arecibo telescope in Puerto Rico. It is far from any major cities to cut interference from other radio sources, such as TV and radio broadcasts and mobile-phone signals.

HOW RADIO TELESCOPES WORK

A radio telescope consists of a curved, reflective dish that collects radio waves from space and focuses it on to an antenna in the centre of the dish. The data picked up is passed to a computer and can be turned into images (as below). The colours shown in these images don't represent the real colours of the objects observed, but show the strength of the radio signal from different parts of the object.

The telescope lies in a depression caused by a sink hole.

ARECIBO OBSERVATORY

CONSTRUCTION	1963 (COMPLETED)
LOCATION	PUERTO RICO
REFLECTOR DIAMETER	305 M (1000.7 FT)

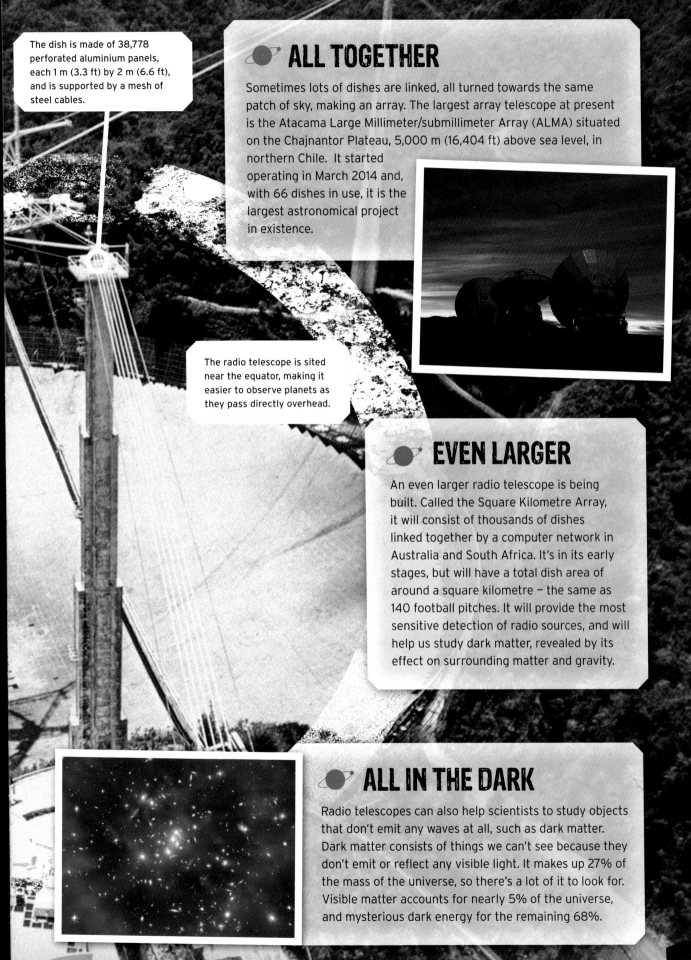

The dish is made of 38,778 perforated aluminium panels, each 1 m (3.3 ft) by 2 m (6.6 ft), and is supported by a mesh of steel cables.

🪐 ALL TOGETHER

Sometimes lots of dishes are linked, all turned towards the same patch of sky, making an array. The largest array telescope at present is the Atacama Large Millimeter/submillimeter Array (ALMA) situated on the Chajnantor Plateau, 5,000 m (16,404 ft) above sea level, in northern Chile. It started operating in March 2014 and, with 66 dishes in use, it is the largest astronomical project in existence.

The radio telescope is sited near the equator, making it easier to observe planets as they pass directly overhead.

🪐 EVEN LARGER

An even larger radio telescope is being built. Called the Square Kilometre Array, it will consist of thousands of dishes linked together by a computer network in Australia and South Africa. It's in its early stages, but will have a total dish area of around a square kilometre – the same as 140 football pitches. It will provide the most sensitive detection of radio sources, and will help us study dark matter, revealed by its effect on surrounding matter and gravity.

🪐 ALL IN THE DARK

Radio telescopes can also help scientists to study objects that don't emit any waves at all, such as dark matter. Dark matter consists of things we can't see because they don't emit or reflect any visible light. It makes up 27% of the mass of the universe, so there's a lot of it to look for. Visible matter accounts for nearly 5% of the universe, and mysterious dark energy for the remaining 68%.

LARGEST RECORDED ASTEROID IMPACT

TUNGUSKA EVENT

Earth has been blasted by lots of asteroids in the past, but the largest one to be recorded in human history happened at Tunguska, Russia, in 1908.

A massive, explosive fireball of blinding light, accompanied by a series of bangs heard 1,000 km (621 miles) away, marked the crash of the asteroid into a remote Siberian forest. The crash registered on seismometers (used to record earthquakes) 1,500 km (932 miles) away. People working at a 30 km (19 miles) distance were hurled into the air, though no one is known to have been killed. The sky filled with dust that glowed with light even after dark.

TUNGUSKA EVENT

DATE	30 JUNE 1908
LOCATION	NEAR THE PODKAMENNAYA TUNGUSKA RIVER, SIBERIA
AREA AFFECTED	2,150 KM² (1,336 MILES²)
LIKELY SIZE	35–40 M (115-131 FT) ACROSS
LIKELY MASS	100 MILLION KG (220.5 MILLION LB)

Eighty million trees were stripped of their branches, burned or flattened over an area 65 km (40 miles) across.

EXPLOSION IN MID-AIR

Scientists modelling the event say a rocky asteroid 35-40 m (115-131 ft) across exploded 6 km (3.7 miles) above the ground. Plunging towards Earth at a speed of 54,000 km/h (33,554 mph), the asteroid would have been heated to around 24,700 °C (44,492 °F) – enough to make it explode into tiny pieces.

GODS AND UFOS

Scientists finally visited the site 20 years after the incident. The local people avoided the blast site for years as they believed a god called Ogdy had destroyed the trees and killed the animals as a punishment for their wickedness. Some people claim the blast was caused by a nuclear-powered UFO exploding before hitting the ground. They give the lack of a crater or pieces of meteorite as evidence – but there are no pieces of UFO either!

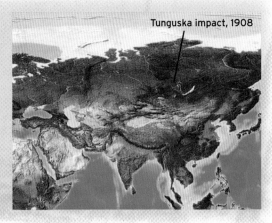

Tunguska impact, 1908

No crater or chunks of meteorite have been found at the site, but tiny fragments of stone that match common meteorites have been found embedded in trees and in a bog nearby.

A BIG LUMP OF METAL

Not all asteroids explode or burn up as they pass through the atmosphere. The largest preserved meteorite is the Hoba meteorite in Namibia. It crashed into southern Africa up to 80,000 years ago. The iron meteorite is the most massive naturally occurring lump of iron on Earth's surface. When it was found, its mass was around 60,000 kg (132,277 lb). There is no crater – it was discovered by a farmer ploughing his field in 1920.

The blast was nearly 200 times as powerful as the nuclear bomb that destroyed the Japanese city of Hiroshima in 1945.

ONLY KNOWN INHABITED PLANET

EARTH

Although there are probably billions of planets in the universe that can support life, the only one that we know is inhabited is our home planet, Earth.

Life on Earth began with single-celled organisms at least three billion years ago. For 2.5 billion years, everything stayed very small and simple, and all life was in the sea. Nothing could see what was happening, as eyes had not evolved! Then around 550 million years ago, life exploded into lots of shapes and sizes. Plants and animals moved on to the land. The variety we see now had begun.

CAN YOU LIVE THERE?

Life on Earth is robust. It has survived six mass extinctions, when most species were wiped out, and re-established in just a few million years. Some creatures – called extremophiles – live in the harshest environments. There is life under the ice sheets, on the tops of mountains, deep underground, within rocks and even inside underwater volcanic vents at temperatures up to 122 °C (251.6 °F).

EARTH

MASS	5.972 X 10^{24} KG (13.166 X 10^{24} LB), ABOUT 6 TRILLION TRILLION KG (13 TRILLION TRILLION LB)
DIAMETER	12,742 KM (7,918 MILES)
DISTANCE FROM SUN	150 MILLION KM (93 MILLION MILES) (1 AU)
MASS OF LIVING THINGS	560,000 BILLION KG (OVER 1,000,000 BILLION LB) (WITHOUT BACTERIA)

Around two thirds of the surface of the Earth is covered by water, and much of that remains unexplored.

There are at least 8.7 million species of animals and plants on Earth – and many more species of bacteria.

INSIDE EARTH

The Earth has a core made mostly of iron, surrounded by a thick mantle of semi-liquid molten rock. The core is as hot as the surface of the Sun! A thin crust of rock floats on top, carrying the continents and oceans. Above is an atmosphere of nitrogen and oxygen. The crust is divided into huge slabs that move very slowly. Rock that was at the seabed millions of years ago is now at the top of mountains – complete with fossils of fish and crabs.

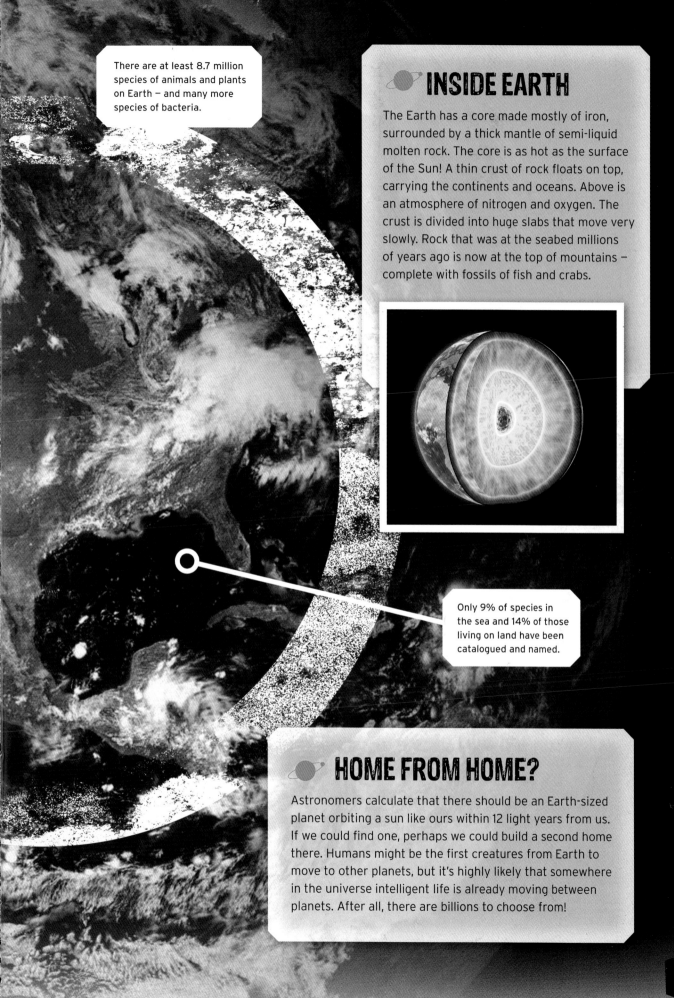

Only 9% of species in the sea and 14% of those living on land have been catalogued and named.

HOME FROM HOME?

Astronomers calculate that there should be an Earth-sized planet orbiting a sun like ours within 12 light years from us. If we could find one, perhaps we could build a second home there. Humans might be the first creatures from Earth to move to other planets, but it's highly likely that somewhere in the universe intelligent life is already moving between planets. After all, there are billions to choose from!

PICTURE CREDITS:
The publishers would like to thank the following sources for their kind permission to reproduce the pictures in this book.

Key: t=top, l=left, r=right, c=centre & b=bottom.

1-3 Thinkstock.com, 6-7 Moment Open/Getty Images, 8-9 University of Copenhagen/Lars Buchhave, 12-13 David Kingham, 12bl Tomasz Stawarz, 13t ESO, 13r myrockman.com, 14 Popperfoto/Getty Images, 14-15 Hulton Archive/Getty Images, 15r U.S. Navy, 20 & 21 Rolls Press/Popperfoto/Getty Images, 22b Library of Congress Prints and Photographs, 22-23

Shutterstock.com, 23t Energia, 24b ESA, 24-25 Ria Novosti/Science Photo Library, 25b ESA, 26-27 Gunnar Hildonen/GuideGunnar, 31b Xinhua/Alamy Xinhua/Alamy, 37t EPA/Yuri Kochetkov/Alamy, 37b Central Press/Getty Images, 38 Roger Ressmeyer/Corbis, 45t Shutterstock, 46b Keystone-France/Gamma-Keystone via Getty Images, 46-47 Keystone/Getty Images, 47t NASA, 51tr Jon Lomberg/Science Photo Library, 52 The Yerkes Observatory, 52-53 Space Frontiers/Hulton Archive/Getty Images, 53l Hulton Archive/Getty Images, 53tr DeAgostini/Getty Images, 53cr Print Collector/Getty Images, 56 & 56-57 Sovfoto/UIG via Getty

Images, 59tr Skatebiker via Wikipedia, 65tr Universal History Archive/UIG via Getty Images, 66b Shutterstock, 66-67 Alexander Nemenov/AFP/Getty Images, 67br Courtesy of Virgin Galactic, 74-75 ESO, 76-77 David A Aguilar, 84bl Keystone/Getty Images, 84-85 & 85b Sovfoto/UIG via Getty Images, 87br Courtesy of Lego, 90-91 ESO, 92 & 92-93 Shutterstock, 93 Mark Pilkington/Geological Survey of Canada/Science Photo Library, 94-95 Corbis, 98-99 ESO, 100 Erik Viktor/AFP/Getty Images, 102bl Bernard Hoffman/Time Life Pictures/Getty Images, 106-107 H.Schweiker/WIYN/NOAO/AURA/NSF 107tr ALMA/ESO/NAOJ, 108-109 Leonid Kulix Expedition, 109t Shutterstock,

109b Eugen Zibiso, 110l © Chris Allen, 111r Shutterstock

All other images supplied by NASA

Every effort has been made to acknowledge correctly and contact the source and/or copyright holder of each picture and Carlton Books Limited apologises for any unintentional errors or omissions, which will be, corrected in future editions of this book.